REDUC[

How do I reduce crime in my police command? How do I tackle chronic crime problems? How do I address the long-term issues that have plagued my community? How do I analyze crime and criminal behavior? How do I show evidence of success in crime reduction? What works, what doesn't, and how do we know?

Providing answers to these questions and more, this engaging and accessible book offers a foundation for leadership in modern policing. Blending concepts from crime science, environmental criminology, and the latest research in evidence-based policing, the book draws on examples from around the world to cover a range of issues such as:

- how to analyze crime problems and what questions to ask
- why the PANDA model is your key to crime reduction
- key features of criminal behavior relevant to police commanders
- the current research on what works in police crime prevention
- why to set up systems to avoid surprises and monitor crime patterns
- how to develop evidence of your effectiveness
- forming a crime reduction plan and tracking progress
- and finally, how to make a wider contribution to the policing field.

Crammed with useful tips, checklists, and advice, including first-person perspectives from police practitioners, case studies, and chapter summaries, this book is essential reading both for police professionals taking leadership courses and promotion exams, and for students engaged with police administration and community safety.

Jerry H. Ratcliffe is a professor and former British police officer who works with police agencies around the world on crime reduction and criminal intelligence strategy. After an ice-climbing accident ended a decade-long career with London's Metropolitan Police, he earned a first-class honors degree and a PhD from the University of Nottingham. He has published over 80 research articles and numerous books on policing and crime reduction, including (also with Routledge) Intelligence-Led Policing. He has been a research advisor to the FBI and the Philadelphia Police Commissioner. The book draws on his more than 30 years' experience working with police services from El Salvador to New Zealand.

"This is an accessible guide for everyday policing. There is a real need for an informed practical approach to leadership practice. It's an easy interesting read, and Ratcliffe deserves some kind of award for collating these checklists. I wish I had had this as a superintendent."

Sir Denis O'Connor, Her Majesty's Chief Inspector of Constabulary (rtd.) and affiliated lecturer, Institute of Criminology, University of Cambridge (U.K.)

"Whether you are just beginning as a police leader or have been in a leadership position for years, 'Reducing Crime' should be the first call for back up when you are faced with a complicated crime problem. Of all the books I have read on crime science, this wins hands down on its ability to explain how to approach problems practically in the complex world of modern day policing. This is a book I would like to see as part of the Police leadership curriculum. The structure of the book and the personal touch of real police leaders' experiences makes it the best I have read."

Bruce O'Brien, Inspector, New Zealand Police

"*Reducing Crime* is a must-read for any senior leader in today's evolving police environment. Twenty-first century policing demands more than the standard reactive-model approaches from decades past. Today's police leaders require more strategic responses to crime prevention, awareness of community harms, and education regarding evidence-based practices. Often missing in today's command level training, this book bridges the gap and should sit as a ready-reference on every commander's desk."

Chris Vallejo, Lieutenant, Austin Police Department, Texas (U.S.)

"I have read the book which is excellent and I only wish I had been able to read this five years ago. It is full of information, reflections, observations and resources that will support any serving police officer either in post or thinking about future roles. I recommend it as a must read for all police professionals. Jerry has done the almost impossible by presenting solid academic material in a format that appeals and is easy to understand and more importantly, put into use."

Inspector Dan Reynolds, Inspector, Cheshire Police (U.K.)

REDUCING CRIME

A COMPANION FOR POLICE LEADERS

JERRY H. RATCLIFFE

Routledge
Taylor & Francis Group

LONDON AND NEW YORK

First published 2019
by Routledge
2 Park Square, Milton Park, Abingdon, Oxon OX14 4RN

and by Routledge
711 Third Avenue, New York, NY 10017

Routledge is an imprint of the Taylor & Francis Group, an informa business

British Library Cataloguing-in-Publication Data
A catalogue record for this book is available from the British Library

Library of Congress Cataloging-in-Publication Data
A catalog record has been requested for this book

ISBN: 978-0-8153-5460-4 (hbk)
ISBN: 978-0-8153-5461-1 (pbk)
ISBN: 978-1-351-13235-0 (ebk)

Typeset in Joanna
by Apex CoVantage, LLC

Visit the companion website: www.reducingcrime.com

CONTENTS

FIGURES

BOXES

TABLES

FOREWORD

I first met Dr. Jerry Ratcliffe in 2008, soon after I became the Police
Commissioner in Philadelphia. He headed the department of criminal
justice at Temple University. It didn't take long before I recognized
his depth of knowledge of policing. What stood out to me was his
perspective was that of a practitioner rather than purely academic. His
latest book is a reflection of that.

Jerry has taken his experience working with police departments in
the United States coupled with his own experience as a police officer
in the United Kingdom and turned it into this remarkable book. It
contains more than 20 vignettes from police officers serving in six
countries. He places a focus on area command with a viable model
that can be used by practitioners in the field. Dr. Ratcliffe also intro-
duces a crime reduction model PANDA, based on the SARA model
used by many departments but expanded for command purposes.

Jerry presents a very complex topic in an easy to understand way.
Greg Brown, CEO of Motorola in discussing his theory of leadership,
provided the following advice to aspiring police chiefs; "Succeed
where you are not where you want to go." Jerry's book is a roadmap
for leaders to succeed where they are and prepares them to move
to the next level. The book focuses on leadership, evidence-based

policing, what police can do, and how crime prevention works. Dr. Ratcliffe has written a must-read for police leaders everywhere.

Charles H. Ramsey
(Ret) Police Commissioner, Philadelphia PD
(Ret) Police Chief, Metropolitan Police Washington, D.C.

ACKNOWLEDGMENTS

Many people provided assistance in the completion of this book and for their help I am truly grateful. Among them, in alphabetical order, are Corey Allen, Katherine Arguenta-Marenco, Jeff Asher, Myrna Avila, Jonas Baughman, Steve Bishopp, Jim Bueermann, Hannah Catterall, Spencer Chainey, Paul Daly, Steve Darroch, Martin Gallagher, Stuart Greer, Shawn Hagan, Emma Harder, Laura Huey, Mike Jenkins, Gordon King, Limehouse Police Facebook group members, Ian MacDonald, Aili Malm, Tarrick McGuire, Pedro Antonio Guillén Meléndez, Colleen Michvech, Ken Michvech, Renée Mitchell, Don Moser, Alex Murray, Arif Navaz, Tom Nestel, Mike Newman, Bruce O'Brien, Sir Denis O'Connor, Andy Parkes, Jared Parkin, Jeff Peake, Roger Pegram, Brian Prescott, Charles Ramsey, Dan Reynolds, Kelly Robbins, Jim Rose, Justin Ross, Tait Sanborn, Dave Spencer, Greg Stewart, Gareth Stubbs, Tom Sutton, Tracey Thompson, Neil Trainor, Chris Vallejo, Julio César Marroquín Vides, and Levin Wheller.

DISCLAIMER

The book includes contributions from numerous individuals. The views and quotes from the vignette authors and any other individual identified in this book are their own and do not necessarily represent their city, county, agency, police service, police force, sheriff's office, country, or police department. Their rank and role at time of publication is shown for information purposes only and should not be construed to indicate or suggest any agency approval, support for, or agreement with any position or opinion stated. Furthermore, their rank, role, and even agency may have changed since publication. Please check the supporting website for updated biographies. As for the rest of the book, any mistakes, omissions, poorly chosen examples, inaccuracies, or other general nonsense are mine alone. I embrace them like old friends with wildly differing political views, in that I secretly hope they will be eradicated by the second edition.

NOTES

Terms displayed like this are explained in a glossary found on the supporting website. The website also contains additional materials and example questions, some graphics from the book in download-able format, and updated links.

The website is reducingcrime.com. You can also subscribe to updates on twitter by following @_reducingcrime (please note the underscore).

1

THE STRATEGIC POLICE LEADER

The core goals of modern policing are clear: prevent crime, increase community safety and security, build public trust and confidence in the police, and do all of this in fair and lawful ways. These objectives were part of the mission when I joined the Metropolitan Police Service in London as a cadet in 1984, and they remain the core mission of policing in a democracy today.[1]

While these core goals have remained consistent, the pace of change since the mid-1980s for everyone in law enforcement has been bewildering. The social service function has taken on a more significant role as funding for other community agencies has diminished. Yet crime fighting remains, in the minds of officers and the public, a core mission of the police.

If you are a serving officer reading this, then keeping people safe, either from crime or other societal harms, is likely why you joined the job. You have experienced the joys, frustrations, boredom, fear, and exhilaration of being a police officer. You and your family are acutely familiar with the commitment and desire to make a difference. But that core mission—actually making a difference—seems harder these days, especially after promotion. The new world of police command takes place in the spotlight. Police leaders, and especially mid-level commanders, are under more scrutiny than ever before. The job has more accountability, and feels more urgent. Unfortunately, these trends can drive a short-termism and a risk aversion that is harmful to good decision-making and, ultimately, public safety.

> *Police leaders, and especially mid-level commanders, are under more scrutiny than ever before.*

While this modern world has created greater accountability, many commanders lack experience in implementing successful crime reduction. Their previous policing roles were often tactical and oriented to discrete cases and solving individual calls for service. This isn't to negate that wealth of experience, but rather to realize that being a commander requires a skill set that is fundamentally different from frontline policing. It is rarely taught and difficult to acquire prior to actually being in command.

I've been lucky enough to consult and work with police commanders from five continents, and there are some commonalities worth mentioning. They might have been promoted on the basis of passing an exam and demonstrating some legal knowledge, or when they demonstrated excellent on-the-ground, incident-driven presence. As new commanders quickly learn, these experiences do not necessarily prepare one for the new craft of policing: working with partners and demonstrating strategic leadership—directing policies and programs. Because agencies have limited training budgets, most area commanders are thrust into command with little preparation.

There is also a general assumption that area commanders know how to 'do' crime reduction, simply by virtue of having been in the job for some years and earning promotion. They may have been detectives, worked in the property or personnel office, or been the liaison to the local counter-terrorism center. The police service often thinks that these disparate jobs qualify someone to be an area commander skilled in planning and organizing burglary and vehicle crime reduction campaigns. This is akin to asking a doctor with expertise in tropical diseases to be the chief surgeon at an inner-city trauma unit. Some basic ideas are common, but in general the previous experiences are of limited value in the new role (as Tracey Thompson explains in Box 1.1).

If this feels familiar, then don't worry—this book has been written for you. Of course, there is no way to predict your exact circumstances precisely; however the aim of this book is to provide a general evidence-driven guide to the challenge of reducing crime in your community.

BOX 1.1 LEADERS SHOULD NOT TAKE FOR GRANTED THE *MANA*

"Although I had 22 years of policing under my belt, this in no way prepared me for the responsibility I faced when I stepped into an area command role. I'd been a technical expert in various police roles, but as area commander it was not as important to know a lot about one thing, but instead to know a little about everything. I needed to be informed enough that I could work with the many audiences I was now required to engage with both internally and externally.

The reality was that for the first few months of my tenure the 'people' aspect of my role seemed to take precedence. Staff were trying to get a sense of my priorities and it was important to me that I was a visible and supportive leader. I do not take for granted the *mana* (our Māori word for prestige, status, and authority) that comes with this role.

Externally, there was also a high expectation of me from our community. My area has a multi-cultural vibrancy, but also great wealth and age divides. And being Māori, it was important for me to build and maintain strong relationships with our local Iwi (tribe) and Māori community. I therefore had to be dynamic in the way I managed the different needs of our diverse communities.

As I got more comfortable in my role, conversations at our leadership table began to change with more focus on achieving our organizational priorities of crime, crash, and victimization prevention. To do this we have continued to build and maintain strategic relationships with our community and government partners. I've learned that leadership is the key to being a good area commander, and it's a long journey."

Tracey Thompson is an inspector with the New Zealand Police. She is currently area commander of Kapiti Mana Police in Wellington District.

A COMMUNITY HARM PERSPECTIVE

As you move into a more strategic leadership role, you will be challenged to micromanage less and adopt a broader perspective. This includes balancing crime and disorder reduction alongside other community and organizational goals, including police legitimacy. As one police colleague told me: "nothing about my previous service prepared me for being a district captain."

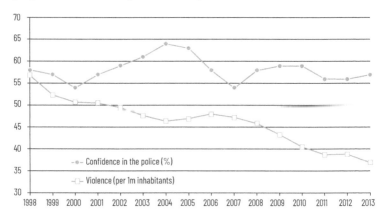

Figure 1.1 Violence compared to confidence in police
Sources: Gallup, FBI UCR Crime in the United States

Policing isn't just about crime. If it were, the police would have reaped a public perception reward for the decades of lowering recorded crime since 1990. Figure 1.1 shows the percentage of American adults who have a 'great deal' or 'quite a lot' of confidence in the police. Alongside is the violent crime rate per one million inhabitants. While crime has steadily declined, that benefit doesn't appear to have changed public perception of the police.

Trust and confidence in law enforcement do not stem from just tackling crime. Modern policing is about delivering a service that addresses harm, social disorder, community safety, and reassurance, all in a framework that instills confidence in the police and is procedurally just. The public want their police to not only fight crime but be attentive to their needs: reliable, responsive, and competent. They also want the police to have good manners, and to treat people with fairness.[2]

> I've worked with area commanders who are judged by the community as much on their ability to combat late-night noise and traffic problems as reducing violence and murder.

Wherever there is crime, there is frequently also physical and social disorder. In some of the most crime-ridden corners of everywhere from Philadelphia to San Salvador, I've worked with area commanders who are judged by the community as much on their ability to combat late-night noise and traffic problems as reducing violence and murder. People worry about crime, but they are also drained by the day-to-day dysfunction in their neighborhoods. While this book focuses on crime, the techniques you will find in here are also useful for dealing with many of these nuisance issues.

A challenge you will certainly face is that others may not share your sense of what is a problem and how to deal with it. With promotion, you will increasingly hear from the mayor, other law enforcement agencies, frontline officers, the police chief, non-governmental organizations, and different factions in the community. You become increasingly exposed to chronic problems that lie beneath the surface of your policing area. You will attend meetings and get briefings that open your eyes to a new viewpoint. You are likely to be more aware of the community's concerns than most patrol and frontline officers, and you will inevitably become a more strategic thinker (see Box 1.2).

This can clash with the perspective of frontline responders who focus on the immediate and seek out pragmatic solutions that work in the moment. As you develop a sense of the problems you need to address, be aware that other stakeholders may not share your perspective. Their goals and aspirations, and even their feelings about the role of the police in modern society, may be fundamentally different. You will likely have to rely on softer skills, persuasion, and transformational leadership to negotiate with these groups (see Chapter 11).

BOX 1.2 DATA FUELS A HOLISTIC APPROACH TO CRIME PROBLEMS

"In policing, we assume that you are immediately competent upon promotion and on arrival in your new role. After all, you've been a cop for many years, so your professional judgement will guide you through, right? This belief couldn't be farther from the truth. When I started as an area commander, vast quantities of detailed information hit my screen with limited explanation. What did it all mean, how was I to decipher it all, and what did I need to do? I was lost in a sea of information with no guidance.

I sought help. I quickly learnt that by sharing crime data with key stakeholders I was able to support a more robust, holistic approach to our crime problems. I used data to focus on not only crime reduction but also building neighborhood cohesion. Before taking an area command, I had never realized how important community and other government partners were in modern policing. Tackling problems together with partnerships provided far wider benefits than I could achieve on my own. In time, communities began to take pride in their area, influencing a reduction in crime and creating a place in which people could have pride."

Jared Parkin is a superintendent in Dorset Police (U.K.), with responsibility for operational and neighborhood policing in an urban environment.

A THREE-PRONGED APPROACH TO CRIME REDUCTION

For police officers with a good nose for crime, the move to command can often be challenging. Charles Ramsey, former Philadelphia Police Commissioner, once said, "You think at first it's just about locking up bad guys, but it's not. It's really about making communities safer."[3] I remembered this quote when I was on a ride-along with officers in a busy inner-city precinct. Their captain had a reputation for patrolling and making arrests, yet these experienced cops lamented that their area didn't feel like it had any kind of a plan to make a dent in crime. They just chased the radio from call to call, without a sense that there was a strategy. While he appreciated the street cop side of his captain, one patrol officer said: "That's not what he is paid for. That's not why he gets the big bucks."

While he appreciated the street cop side of his captain, one patrol officer said "That's not what he is paid for. That's not why he gets the big bucks."

Good street cops have a natural tendency to get into the weeds. It's not necessarily the best trait for a leader. Without a strategic plan we are left with fire-brigade policing, rushing from call to call yet doing little to address chronic problems strategically. Sir Denis O'Connor served as one of Britain's most senior police officers (after getting his start on H district in the Metropolitan Police). He refers to much of current policing as 'schoolboy football.' If you have ever watched youngsters playing soccer, you will know what he means. They all crowd around the ball and whenever it moves somewhere else on the pitch, they all rush there. Police officers have a similar level of enthusiasm, energy, and passion to not only get stuck in but also to make them feel good about themselves. Management meetings that rush to address problems yet lack any strategic perspective (such as most Compstat-type meetings) are often the mechanism by which we police like schoolboy football. Every month the red dots move a bit, and every month we rush to move our blue dots.

To help overcome this, the book stresses a deliberate process to focus on three crime reduction priorities:

- address crime hot spots
- engage in proactive policing
- reduce criminal opportunities.

These are not priorities based on weak predilection. These focal areas have robust empirical research that supports giving them particular attention. For example, addressing crime hot spots is a proven crime reduction strategy. Proactive policing recognizes that 6 percent of the population commit 60 percent of the crime. And problem-oriented approaches have been shown to be highly effective. More than 90 percent of police departments use hot spots, offender-focused, and problem-oriented policing for crime-fighting.[4] By focusing on these core areas we can provide some mission clarity to patrol officers, design their work to be more productive, and have a 'plan to win.'[5]

More than 90 percent of police departments use hot spots, offender-focused, and problem-oriented policing for crime fighting.

I certainly recognize that there is value in more long-term social involvement, such as early childhood intervention. As a society, teaching uninformed parents of high-risk kids how to socialize their children and inculcate them with some self-control would likely be a cost-effective mechanism to generate crime reduction benefits in years to come. But these investments do not produce results in a time frame that can help an area commander under pressure from executive leadership and the community. They are also outside of the realm where many police officers feel able to exert influence. The police can do little about parental behavior.

In this book, the focus on crime hot spots, offender-focused proactive interventions, and problem-oriented solutions that reduce opportunities are all areas that resonate with area commanders as being both potentially 'doable' and within their control. The aim is to help you break free from the inefficient and often ineffective cycle of schoolboy football, and we get there with the PANDA model.

THE PANDA MODEL

When I started as a teenage police officer back in the Paleolithic era, sergeants and inspectors were often admired for being assertive and decisive, going with their gut, and not over-complicating things. Find a quick solution, do what we've always done, and don't overthink it. Policing embraced a certain anti-intellectualism and harbored a suspicion of 'thinkers.' Having a university degree was not career-enhancing. While this attitude is slowly changing, it is still prevalent in many police departments. I recall a room full of coppers laughed in wry agreement when Sara Thornton, Chair of the National Police Chiefs' Council, commented drolly that "policing is the only business where the term 'clever' isn't a compliment."

There's no denying the appeal: Cut to the chase, show them who's the boss, enforce the law, and move on to the next call. Unfortunately, offenders and crime problems rarely behave. They don't just slink away, never to return. Unless the issue is clearly understood and a solution that is targeted to the specific cause is properly implemented, real change doesn't happen. Sure, a quick crime suppression operation can temporarily alleviate the issue. But we simply kick the can down the road for someone else to deal with later. The next commander inherits the problem and tries an equally ill-conceived operation. Once again, a momentary clampdown alleviates the concern and the problem is deferred once again. Eventually everyone thinks that nothing can be done, because "everything has been tried." We get stuck in an endless cycle of lather, rinse, and repeat (see Box 1.3, and Box 11.3 in the last chapter).

It is said that Albert Einstein was once asked what he would do if he had just one hour to save the world. His reply was: "I'd spend 55 minutes thinking about the problem and 5 minutes thinking about solutions." This anecdote might be apocryphal; however, the underlying idea is insightful. I worry that a lot of the time in policing we spend 5 minutes analyzing the problem (at most) and 55 minutes continually running operations that rarely work.

BOX 1.3 PULL YOURSELF 'OUT OF THE FLOW'

"We get locked into the cycle of doing, and then doing again, despite the fact that it didn't work in the first place. As a shift leader I would constantly deploy my resources to the same incidents, dealing with the same individuals experiencing the same problems. The drain on the people that I led was severe, and in the midst of this were serious victims who were at risk of coming to real harm. How do you stop that cycle? You have to recognize it first, and then resolve to change it.

One such pattern was repeated calls to a young and vulnerable missing child. I began to see the same complaints raised by the troops: "Why are we going again?" and "She will just go missing again straight away." We were too busy to ask the important question: "How do we stop this happening again?" As an agency, we weren't addressing any of the root problems.

When we found her in the company of a registered sex offender, we put the non-urgent calls on hold and spent five hours with the missing girl. Only then did she disclose a history of familial abuse and neglect. Those few hours were worth another 100 or more that would have been repeatedly spent by shift after shift. To solve the problem, we had to understand the problem. We had to pull ourselves out of the flow and try to understand what was actually happening. My approach ruffled some feathers, but I know I'm making an actual difference now, and that matters."

Gareth Stubbs is an inspector with Lancashire Police (U.K.) currently assigned to a team developing evidence-based practice with frontline policing.

Now, if you are from one of the many police forces and departments that has suffered from significant budget cuts and austerity over the last few years, you may be rolling your eyes right now: "How is it possible to slow down when we are run ragged?!" Even with crime lower than previous years, there are more demands on the police and there's no doubt that times are tough. Asking the police service to 'do more with less' has almost become a trite phrase trotted out by politicians unwilling to ask the public to contribute more to their own safety.

The ideas in this book are not a silver bullet that will solve all of your policing resource challenges. There's no doubt that it will be tough to get some people to acknowledge that dealing with even a few of the chronic problems in your area will actually free up resources. Demonstrating that planning before acting, and assessing the return on investment from your limited resources, is the role of a modern police leader.

> On many days, you will have to balance your crime reduc-
> tion objectives with the perpetual routine of response policing
> to individual calls for service. You might also have to balance
> community activities that build relationships and police trust
> and legitimacy.

To help you, PANDA is a mechanism that helps overcome the schoolboy football tendency, and help you be not only personally effective, but also *strategically* effective. The next chapters will introduce you to the model. PANDA is not a model for emergency calls or frontline response policing. It's not designed to deal with your responses to single incidents, though some of the lessons from evidence-based policing can help (see Chapter 10). On many days, you will have to balance your crime reduction objectives with the perpetual routine of frontline response policing. You might also have to balance community activities that build relationships and police trust and legitimacy. But if you want to have an impact on crime, then shifting existing thinking will be necessary. Inspector Gareth Stubbs' tale in Box 1.3 is an example of changing thinking for a chronic problem at a street policing level. Likewise, PANDA is designed for problems and issues that you will increasingly see as you step back a little from the front line and take a long hard look at the business you are now leading.

For demonstration purposes, the main focus of the book and the PANDA model is the need to reduce crime (such as burglary or vehicle theft) in urban and suburban communities. I recognize that there is a vital urgency to address many other areas of criminal activity and police business. Incorporating a community policing perspective and enhancing procedural justice are important in advancing police trust and legitimacy. There is also a growing need to tackle cybercrime, child exploitation, and transnational crime. But, for the sake of brevity, we will focus on the needs of an area commander responsible for the problems in a geographic area. You will, however, find that the principles and skills developed on the way are also effective when addressing other areas of police concern.

A quick note on terminology

Though I spent time on patrol in Central London and with the Diplomatic Protection Group, the majority of my service was on H district at Limehouse in the east end of London. It was a great training ground for the business of policing. To give you a sense of my policing start, it seemed to have changed little in my day from when celebrated detective Frederick Wensley joined the service in the late 1880s and started in the same place (see Box 1.4). My boss was a chief superintendent, the buck-stop for all policing issues in the district; however, across the broad domain of global policing the area commander can have many names such as superintendent, captain, major, inspector, lieutenant, senior sergeant, or sub-comisionado. In some jurisdictions the area is a local policing unit, division, service area, beat, patrol, precinct, delegation, district, or neighborhood policing area. For convenience, I'll be using the general term 'area commander' to refer to the officer responsible for a geographic region. In general, the area commander is a sworn police officer responsible and answerable to the community and executives at police headquarters for the crime and disorder in a geographic area of your jurisdiction. They are the one who rises to respond to the police chief or commissioner in Compstat-type crime management meetings, and the person who is named on a web page as the local leader and point of contact for the community.

BOX 1.4 POLICING THE EAST END OF LONDON

I got my start in the east end of London, like many coppers before me. One of the most famous was Frederick Wensley, who joined the 'Met' in 1887 and also spent much of his career in H district. In a distinguished career with over 40 years in the job, Wensley rose to be

Chief Constable of the Criminal Investigation Department at Scotland Yard. In his first year of service, however, he patrolled the nooks and crannies of H district with rubber strips nailed to his boots in an effort to catch Jack the Ripper. He described the area in a way that resonated with my experiences nearly 100 years later:

"Most of the inhabitants of my new division considered that they had a natural right to get fighting drunk and knock a policeman about whenever the spirit moved them. Bruises and worse were our routine lot. Gangs of hooligans infested the streets and levied blackmail on timorous shopkeepers. There was an enormous amount of personal robbery with violence. The maze of narrow ill-lighted alleys offered easy ways of escape after a man had been knocked down and his watch and money stolen. It was no picnic for a young police officer, but at least it was never dull. You never knew what might happen."[6]

THE STRUCTURE OF THIS BOOK

Whenever you meet someone new, they always have an opinion on how policing should be done. It's usually at a party where the last thing you want to talk about is being in 'the job.' They bring a perspective that is influenced by their experiences, peers, political leanings, viewpoint on offenders, and opinions on the role of the police. Because everyone has a particular bias, let me be transparent about mine. My views on policing and crime reduction are influenced by over a decade as a police officer in London's Metropolitan Police, years as a policing and crime researcher working in the U.K., Australia, New Zealand, Central America, and the United States, and my enthusiasm for pragmatic crime reduction solutions that have some evidence supporting their use. I've been fortunate that this hasn't been just desk work but also extensive field research involving management meetings, ride-alongs, foot patrols, and presence at more than a few arrests. I'm agnostic about most political perspectives on crime in society and try as hard as possible to avoid bringing any particular ideology to this book from either the left or the right. As a crime scientist, I value testing community safety and harm reduction ideas from inside or outside criminal justice, as long as any impacts in terms of legitimacy and democratic values are understood.

I'm immensely grateful to everyone I've had contact with over more than 30 years who has been generous enough to share their experiences, studies, opinions, and thoughts. You will read some of their perspectives integrated into the book, and in the short vignettes. These have been combined with practical academic research to bring you a combination of research-driven, evidence-based, practitioner-designed advice on reducing crime.

Chapters 2, 3, and 4 explain the PANDA framework and describe some simple checklists to get you through the first two parts (the P and A of PANDA) in more detail. Before you nominate your crime reduction strategy (Chapter 7), Chapters 5 and 6 provide some theoretical and practical knowledge necessary to form a good plan. Chapters 8 and 9 describe the last parts of PANDA (deploying a strategy, and assessing the outcome of your operation). The last two chapters (10 and 11) provide an overview of how you can use and develop evidence-based policing and employ management and leadership skills at the local area level. Evidence-based policing is especially important because there is still much to learn about how police can reduce crime. When challenged if their chosen strategy will work, we will move forward when more commanders respond: "I don't know—let's find out!"

Finally, a website has been created for this book containing supporting materials, updates, and further reading. You can find it at: reducingcrime.com. You should check this website for updates to the research knowledge regarding various tactics discussed in later chapters.

The future of policing is harm-focused, intelligence-led, problem-oriented, and evidence-based. This book aims to help you with these strategies. And while at this early stage this may seem a lot to take in, don't forget the simple words of Patrick Colquhoun, who claimed in his *Treatise on the Police* written in 1796, that: "Wherever a proper police attaches . . . good order and security will prevail."[7]

CHAPTER SUMMARY

- The core goals of modern policing are clear: prevent crime, increase community safety and security, build public trust and confidence in the police, and do all of this in fair and lawful ways.
- Being an area commander requires a skill set that is fundamentally different than frontline policing.
- In this book, area commander is a general term used to refer to any police officer responsible for crime in a geographical area.
- Modern policing is about delivering a service that addresses harm, social disorder, community safety, and reassurance, all in a framework that instills confidence in the police and is procedurally just.
- The book stresses a deliberate process to focus on three crime reduction priorities; address crime hot spots, engage in proactive policing, and reduce criminal opportunities.
- Following the PANDA model will momentarily slow down our response and give ourselves time to consider a more careful and measured plan.
- The future of policing is harm-focused, intelligence-led, problem-oriented, and evidence-based.
- Supporting materials can be found at reducingcrime.com.

REFERENCES

1 Lum, C. and D.S. Nagin, *Reinventing American policing*. Crime and Justice, 2017. **46**(1): p. 339–93.

2 Mastrofski, S.D., *Policing for People*. 1999, Police Foundation: Washington, D.C.

3 Kerkstra, P., *Riding with Police Commissioner Charles Ramsey*. 2014, Philadelphia Magazine, posted 30 October, https://www.phillymag.com/articles/2014/10/30/riding-with-police-commissioner-charles-ramsey/.

4 Police Executive Research Forum, *Future Trends in Policing*. 2014, Office of Community Oriented Policing Services: Washington, D.C.

5   O'Connor, D., *The Importance of a Plan to Win*, in *Sir Denis O'Connor's valedictory lecture.* 2012, Her Majesty's Inspectorate of Constabulary. p. 1–9.

6   Wensley, F.P., *Forty Years of Scotland Yard.* 1931, New York: Doubleday, Doran and Company.

7   Colquhoun, P., *A Treatise on the Police of the Metropolis.* 1796, London: J. Mawman.

2

THE PANDA CRIME REDUCTION MODEL

A FRAMEWORK FOR CRIME REDUCTION

BOX 2.1 TWO APPROACHES TO A MEDICAL ISSUE

Imagine walking into your doctor's surgery with an upset stomach. The doctor glances up and says: "I'll prep for surgery." Horrified, you recoil, but the doctor continues: "Don't worry, I've been in this job for twenty years. This is what we always do for an upset stomach." Rapidly going pale you ask: "Will it work?" The doctor snorts, saying, "I have no idea—I don't read the research or follow-up with my other patients. But it's what my mentor did, it's what my predecessors did, and it's what all my colleagues do." This is akin to the traditional model of crime fighting in many places.

These days we assume that the doctor will perform a thorough initial examination (or scan) of the problem to confirm the issue is a serious stomach ache and not something else. If confirmed, then the doctor might send us for some tests or an ultrasound to better analyze the nature of the problem. With more information, we would hope the doctor recommends a specific course of treatment or sends us to a specialist.

It wouldn't be unreasonable to expect that any treatment had been tested on previous sufferers and could be shown to be beneficial (in other words, evidence-based). After the doctor confirms we undertook the treatment, then follow-up tests and our experience would determine if the strategy had been successful. If not, we would certainly hope that the doctor doesn't just throw her hands up in despair. Instead, our learned medic returns to the analysis stage to determine a better course of treatment. This is, in essence, the PANDA model.

Effective and long-term crime reduction doesn't usually happen by accident. It is the result of a process rather than haphazard random activities. Procedures that provide some structure to reducing crime are important because they provide avenues for improvement. We develop processes that include mechanisms for learning and feedback. These drive innovation, change, and improvement. They help enhance knowledge and formalize decision-making.

Before you simply scan Box 2.3, think to yourself "got it—that's easy," and close the book, here's something to consider. Are there crime problems in your patch that were problems before you arrived? Perhaps one or two have been problematic since you joined the department. No doubt your predecessor and his predecessor before him thought that they brought the necessary skill set.

But you probably have fewer resources than they did, and the problems are more entrenched and complex. The traditional policing approach of near-universal dependence on patrol and enforcement as the panacea for all ills is increasingly difficult to sustain. And when you pause and think about it for a moment, a 'one-size-fits-all' approach seems a little ridiculous (see Box 2.1). Yet this is still the dominant model of policing for most of the world.

Fortunately, innovative commanders are looking for fresh approaches to long-term problems. They recognize that a reliance on saturation patrol drains their capacity, limits their deployment options, and—worst of all—rarely works. Even when it does, the benefits of these hit-and-run deployments don't last long. The PANDA model is a checklist designed to help you break this cycle.

BOX 2.2 CHECKLISTS FOR BURGLARY INVESTIGATIONS

"I'd been a police officer for sixteen years when I was introduced to the idea of checklists. I'd never made the connection to using them in policing, simply because it was something I had never been exposed to in any of my training. As a detective supervisor, I wanted to get better outcomes in burglary investigations. Because the initial report from the patrol officers often lacked key details, we simply did not know if key solvability factors were present at burglaries, so lost a lot of time following up on cases that had very little chance of being cleared. I thought a checklist might be worth trying and provided the initial responding officer with a quick reference at the scene so that they could gather better information. The hope was we could make better case-screening decisions when the reports made it to detectives.

Few people want to change what they do, but despite this, it all comes back to the basics. If you can show you have a tool that will help cops be better at their job, there is a chance for success. When our officers used the checklist, they didn't miss important information. When more questions were asked at the scene, more critical information was recorded in the narrative. As a result, the quality of case screening improved, and our detectives were able to focus on more productive cases—to the benefit of the community and the department."

Stuart Greer is currently a lieutenant in charge of the Criminal Investigations Unit with the Morristown, New Jersey, Police Department (U.S.)

CHECKLISTS AND MEMORY AIDS

- I've been flying airplanes since 1999. My first lesson was in an ultralight with an engine that sounded like a hairdryer, flying around a grass paddock outside Goulburn in rural Australia. Since then, I've owned a couple of seaplanes and have an instrument rating, essential when flying through rain and bad weather. These flying experiences have taught me to appreciate checklists and memory aids as vital for both preventing mistakes and improving performance.

Pilots use checklists to reduce complexity. If you think about it, landing an airplane is challenging, even though every time we fly on commercial planes we assume the person up front has everything in hand. The aircraft is moving quickly through three dimensions and you have to touch down at a set speed and attitude, with the aircraft configured correctly for the wind and conditions. This means if you are landing on water the wheels must be up, and if you are landing on a short runway you must get the airspeed down to the slowest safe speed possible. Now imagine doing this in rain and clouds when you can't see beyond the wingtip. All this adds complexity and a considerable 'task load' onto the pilot.

Memory aids and acronyms reduce this complexity to a manageable or memorable set of ordered tasks. They ensure flight crews don't inadvertently skip an important instrument setting or control input. Professions such as aviation and the medical field have developed checklists when practitioners have realized that a series of steps are necessary to prevent failure. Along with engineering improvements, the introduction of efficiency and consistency through systems like checklists has helped to make aviation one of the safest ways to travel today. They are now so commonplace in medicine that some doctors complain that their checklists are too long. Ninety-five percent of those same doctors, however, said that if they were having surgery, they would want all of the items performed![1]

You may be familiar with using risk assessment forms that sometimes resemble checklists. Examples include the DASH (domestic abuse, stalking, and harassment) or MARAC responses to domestic abuse assessments. The checklists in this book are much simpler, and more resemble mnemonics or quick memory aids. No one size fits all, and you should be prepared to tweak the advice from this book to fit your situation. As Aiden Sidebottom and his colleagues point out, they are neither a failsafe nor "should they be followed with slavish orthodoxy."[2] Checklists are, however, a great way to structure thinking and learning about problems, their analysis, and their solutions. And they can be applied to many areas of the job (for example Box 2.2).

The PANDA model is the first checklist or memory aid. The items represent *Problem, Analyze, Nominate, Deploy,* and *Assess,* and each stage is described in the book (and expanded on in Box 2.3). The items can also be referred to as *Problem scan, Analyze problem, Nominate strategy, Deploy strategy,* and *Assess outcomes.* This book will explain these steps in more detail.

BOX 2.3 PANDA CRIME REDUCTION APPROACH

P	**Problem** scan	Clearly scan, describe, and frame the problems in your area. Select priorities for attention.
A	**Analyze** problem	Establish what is known and not yet understood about the prioritized issues, and what needs to be learned. You form a mission at this stage—the goal you want to achieve.
N	**Nominate** strategy	Nominate a VIPER strategy to address victim support, intelligence gaps, prevention, enforcement, and reassurance.
D	**Deploy** strategy	Deploy your strategy with objectives, geography, time frame, and assignment of people responsible for leading, implementing, and analyzing.
A	**Assess** outcomes	Assess the success of your deployment and project outcomes, and consider next steps.

As explained in the opening chapter, this model is not a paradigm shift from other models you might have learned elsewhere. It is not the aim of this book to promote a radical departure from other SARA-type models. Instead, the goal here is to better articulate and describe the steps needed, and pitfalls you might encounter, as you become a crime fighting area commander.

Now more than ever, we need to be a little more scientific in our thinking. As Thomas Huxley wrote in 1880: "There are hardly any of our trades, except the merely huckstering ones, in which some knowledge of science may not be directly profitable to the pursuer of that occupation."[3] The PANDA model brings a little bit of the scientific process to reducing crime.

PANDA is a command-driven, problem-solving model for crime, harm, and disorder concerns.

THE ROLE OF PANDA IN YOUR JOB

PANDA has its origins in similar structural approaches to decision-making you may already be familiar with, such as the SARA model of problem-oriented policing[4] and the 3-i intelligence-led policing model (and a 4-i version you will find in Chapter 4).[5] Each of these tries to inject more structure and logical thinking into crime and disorder reduction. When designing a related model, senior police commanders Roger Gaspar and Brian Flood recognized it was "an ideal model for the whole business of policing that would enable police commanders to understand and anticipate risks and threats across the public safety domain."[6] You should consider the model here in the same way. PANDA is a command-driven, problem-solving model for crime, harm, and disorder concerns.

In much the same way that aviation authorities have a process for investigating aircraft accidents and the scientific method is used to advance numerous scientific fields, the PANDA model is a broad approach designed to be used in a wide variety of policing applications. Like so many problem-solving processes, it follows a simple structure. Define the problem—gather knowledge—identify and deploy a solution—see if the solution worked. While this book focuses on the sort of crime problems likely to be encountered by an area commander in charge of a geographic district (burglary, street crime, disorder, and so forth), PANDA can be used to address other problems in policing, such as recruitment challenges, traffic accident hot spots, officer-involved shootings, or cybercrime. It is similar to SARA but is more specific about strategies and the command structures necessary to implement crime fighting, especially at the *Nominate* and *Deploy* stages. As you can see from the more detailed picture of the PANDA approach in Box 2.4, it has greater specificity in each stage.

BOX 2.4 THE PANDA CRIME REDUCTION APPROACH IN MORE DETAIL

P	Problem scan			Chronic? Spike? Panic?	Long term (months or years)? Short-term flare-up in crime? Possible signal crime or public panic?
A	Analyze problem	V O L T A G E	Victims Offenders Locations Times Attractors Groups Enhancers	What patterns of victimization are evident? What do we know/not know about offenders? What are the characteristics of the places? Significant temporal trends or hot times? Specific places where crime clusters? Any gangs or groups of victims involved? What role for drugs, alcohol, mental health?

N	Nominate strategy	V	Victim support	Any specific activities that can aid victims?
		I	Intelligence gaps	Who can be tasked to fill intelligence gaps?
		P	Prevention	What can be done without police resources?
		E	Enforcement	Where can focused police enforcement help?
		R	Reassurance	Are public reassurance activities needed?
D	Deploy strategy	G	Ground commander	Who will be responsible for implementation?
		O	Objectives	What are the project objectives?
		A	Analyst	Who will monitor and analyze data?
		L	Limits	Spatial and temporal extents of the project?
		S	Support	Additional support needed?
A	Assess outcomes	O	Outcomes achieved?	Were your original outcomes achieved?
		I	Implemented?	Was project implemented as planned?
		L	Lessons learned?	What additional lessons have been learned?
		R	Results?	Are the results acceptable?
		I	Intelligence?	Any useful intelligence gained?
		G	GOALS to be revised?	Do your GOALS need to be revised?

For now, the process stops at the *Assess* stage (see Figure 2.1). The purpose of assessing your outcomes is to determine if you were successful, and if not, why not. At that point, the next steps are determined by the assess stage. We deal with different outcomes later in the book.

There is no expectation that you will use the PANDA approach for all of your area problems. Common sense needs to be applied. If your patrol car runs out of fuel, a quick trip to the gas station will suffice. But you might be surprised how the introduction of some structured thinking can enhance your professional work practice. Even if you don't deploy the whole PANDA model, the components can be useful. For example, if your community policing officer returns from a meeting and complains that the gathering was a failure, it might be useful to run through a couple of the OILRIG checklist items from the assess stage. Before declaring failure, what were the proposed outcomes of the meeting? You can sometimes find that meeting objectives were never clearly set. Ambiguity or a lack of specificity invites failure.

As you proceed through the book, you will also be encouraged to consider the role of PANDA outside of crime fighting. As an instrument-rated pilot, even though I can fly the aircraft entirely by the dials and gauges, my instructors have always encouraged me to look out of the windshield. As former police chief Jim Bueermann points out, what he has always looked for in an area commander is a balance of crime reduction and community concern (Box 2.5).

BOX 2.5 A POLICE CHIEF'S PERSPECTIVE ON GOOD
AREA COMMAND

"When I counsel a new area commander, I first let them know that I want them to succeed and do better than I did when I was a lieutenant! Be responsive to the community and benefit from my mistakes. I also ask that they focus on three things. First, it's not only the traditional indicators of crime but also the risk factors that contribute to harm in the community. The community doesn't care what the national crime labels are. They care about those things and people in their neighborhoods that affect their quality of life and put their kids at risk.

Second, co-produce public safety with the people of your area command. This means stakeholders in the community and the cops and crime analysts that work for you. These groups know a lot about crime. Listen to them individually and collectively. Make safety in your command a joint responsibility of the community and the police department.

Finally, know your community. Get out and walk the streets. Develop a healthy aversion to being in your office. Ride with patrol officers at different times and days. Meet the business owners, school officials, and community advocates. Become the expert on your command. The perception about safety of people who live in your command area is now your reality. In the final analysis, only people count."

Jim Bueermann was the police chief in Redlands, California (U.S.) for 13 years. He is currently the president of the Police Foundation.

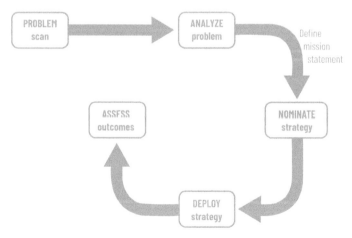

Figure 2.1 **The PANDA model**

For most problems that are not an easy fix, and even for some that might appear to be, the full PANDA model is recommended (see Figure 2.1). The next chapters detail each of the PANDA stages, going into more detail with specific checklist items in each.

CHAPTER SUMMARY

- The PANDA items are *Problem scan*, *Analyze problem*, *Nominate strategy*, *Deploy strategy*, and *Assess outcomes*.
- They can also be referred to as *Problem*, *Analyze*, *Nominate*, *Deploy*, and *Assess*.
- PANDA is a command-driven, problem-solving model for crime, harm, and disorder concerns.
- PANDA can be applied to a wide range of problems, not just crime and disorder issues.
- For problems that are not an easy and immediate fix, the full model is recommended.

REFERENCES

1   Powell, A., *Checklists are boring, but death is worse*. Harvard Gazette, 2017. October 16. Online at https://news.harvard.edu/gazette/story/2017/10/checklists-are-boring-but-death-is-worse/

2   Sidebottom, A., N. Tilley, and J.E. Eck, *Towards checklists to reduce common sources of problem-solving failure*. Policing: A Journal of Policy and Practice, 2012. **6**(2): p. 194–209.

3   Huxley, T.H., *The practical value of science*. Science, 1880. **1**(1): p. 3.

4   Eck, J.E. and W. Spelman, *Problem-solving: Problem-oriented policing in Newport News*. 1987, Police Executive Research Forum: Washington, D.C.

5   Ratcliffe, J.H., *Intelligence-Led Policing (2nd edition)*. 2016, Abingdon, Oxon.: Routledge.

6   Flood, B. and R. Gaspar, *Strategic aspects of the UK National Intelligence Model*, in *Strategic Thinking in Criminal Intelligence (2nd edition)*, J.H. Ratcliffe, Editor. 2009, Federation Press: Sydney. p. 47–65.

3

PROBLEM SCANNING

THE VIEW FROM PATTERN ALTITUDE

I love taking people flying for the first time. There is a moment just after the plane leaves the runway when the passenger has an involuntary grin on their face. The miracle of flight becomes real as the ground drops away. There is a reason that a light aircraft flight can't be beaten as a first date! That initial reaction is soon replaced by a sense of awe. From only ever seeing the streets from the ground, my passenger now sees the entire neighborhood. They can, for the first time, appreciate how large the shopping center is, or how many trees cover their community. The scale changes, features and patterns are recognized, and new connections are made. It really does change one's perspective.

You may have experienced one viewpoint from a commercial jet in flight. Senior executives talk about seeing their business from 30,000 feet, where a chief can use this overview to get a handle on the entire policing challenge. For example, consider Figure 3.1.[1] The size of each box is a proportion of the more than 1.5 million incidents in the U.S. city of Philadelphia each year. While the media panics about changes in the violent crime rate, these are relatively negligible in terms of incident volume. Even for a city with

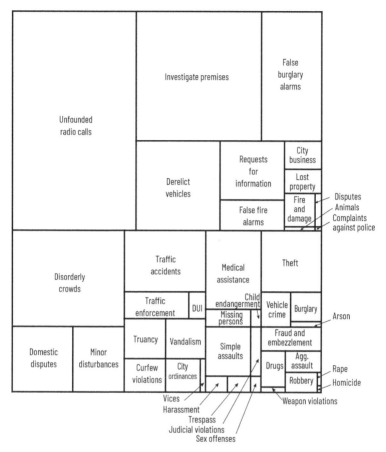

Figure 3.1 One year of incidents by volume for Philadelphia

a reputation for violence, consider how much time is consumed by the other neighborhood harms. They often indicate what truly bothers the wider community and what may need significant attention.

If you are at a mid-level command rank, you need to be closer to the problem. This is where pattern altitude is useful. When pilots approach an airfield, they fly around the area in a prescribed route at about 1,000 feet above the runway. This is called pattern altitude, the height at which we fly in the airplane 'traffic pattern'. It is high enough to see the entire airfield and the full scope of the environment, but it is also close enough to inspect the runway and locate other aircraft. Sometimes I fly to a new airport and from pattern altitude notice deer on the runway. They can't be seen from 30,000 feet.

A problem scan is your view from pattern altitude. It is the first stage in the PANDA model. *Problem scan* is a term adapted from the business world (environmental scan) but in policing it means to gather information about the problems, challenges, and threats to your community. It sits between case-specific investigations (tactical) and executive level planning (strategic). This pattern altitude is where operational police leadership resides. It might tell you that your area differs from the city-wide aggregate picture or if your local context is substantially different. You may need to engage with your community directly to identify why your area has challenges that are dissimilar to the rest of the city. It could also bolster your case to take a fresh approach from that of your colleagues.

When you start somewhere as the area commander, it will be useful to either conduct your own problem scan or—or if you are lucky—task a crime analyst to help you put together a problem scan. It is a needs assessment tool to aid you in figuring out where the significant problems are and where you should focus your attention and concentrate your resources. Pilots fly a regular route in the 'traffic pattern.' This standardized path ensures everyone knows what each pilot is doing and it reinforces good practice and safe flying. In the chapters that follow you will find a couple of checklists to help you develop a similar routine approach to problem scans and analysis.

Think about wider harms and community threats

Policing has undergone significant changes since I graduated from Hendon Police College. One of the more recent has been a move towards harm-focused policing, which "weighs the social harms of criminality and disorder with data from beyond crime and antisocial behavior, in order to focus police priorities and resources in furtherance of both crime *and* harm reduction."[2] The issues you will likely have to deal with extend far beyond crime and into community safety and harm reduction. Police departments now spend more time than ever on harm reduction, dealing with people suffering behavioral health episodes, chronic drug users, problem families, traffic and crash reduction, and juveniles in conflict. As explained by Corey Allen in Box 3.1, dealing with these issues requires police leaders to reflect on procedural justice when dealing with social harms. This emphasizes the nature of police interactions and how police treat the public during everyday encounters and normal police work. It is believed to be linked to the public's perception of police legitimacy (more on procedural justice and police legitimacy in Chapter 11).

BOX 3.1 ADDRESSING BRISBANE'S SOCIAL HARMS

"When newly appointed in charge of Brisbane City station it was quickly obvious that crime was only one factor affecting big city policing. Our performance reporting focused on crime and detections, but the issues plaguing frontline police and the community were quite different. Homelessness, young people in conflict, and the degeneration of newly built yet poorly managed social housing were the big priorities for officers.

It took some convincing but eventually the command let us work on vulnerable persons as a key strategy. We developed partnerships to help frontline officers engage and divert people from custody. Now frontline police could offer referral to support services at any time, including to those we arrested or dealt with as usual business. By being able to ask, 'what is the problem here?' rather than just arrest, we became more procedurally just. The officer on the beat could connect vulnerable persons to support services instead of a night in the cells.

Our rates of arrest for minor offences dropped. The people we referred became less prone to assault police, and we saw reductions in obstruct and resist police charges. Our levels of assault on police reduced from 135 per year to 35 per year over seven years, sick leave

improved, and we performed significantly better than similar neighboring divisions. The time we recouped was invested in more traditional police business but more significantly the attitude and culture
of the officers started to improve."

Corey Allen is an inspector with the Queensland Police
Service (Australia) and is currently the manager of opera-
tional training services. He was formerly the officer in
charge of Queensland's largest station, Brisbane City.

Try to incorporate in your scan a measure of the harm of incidents rather than just the frequency of narrow categories of crimes.
Remember that public concerns such as disorderly behavior, disturbances, traffic problems, and even graffiti are also a huge drain on
police resources and time (see Figure 3.1). The page supporting this
chapter at the book's website (reducingcrime.com) has more information on harm-focused policing.

THE PROBLEM SCAN

A problem scan is your starting point to figuring out where your
priorities should be. There is no way to write the perfect book for
everyone in modern policing, as your work environment may not
reflect exactly what has been laid out here. As the caveat for new car
fuel consumption warns, your mileage may differ. But, in general,
there are some common useful areas. The aim is to identify recurring
problems that are concerns to the public and the police. The lists in
Box 3.2 are not exhaustive nor do you have to include them all if
some are not relevant; however, they may help you get started in
terms of categories to explore.

BOX 3.2 EXAMPLE CATEGORIES AND HEADINGS FOR A PROBLEM SCAN

Community
Demographic trends
Urban trends
Business investment/sentiment
Public perception
Legislative and political impacts

Crime
Property crime
Violent crime
Internet and cyber crime
Drug-related crime
Organized crime
Gangs
Problem places

Traffic
Traffic crime
Traffic accidents
Transit crime
Congestion

Vulnerable populations
Youth crime and victimization
Elderly crime
Tourist victimization
Domestic abuse and violence
Mental health
Homelessness
Troubled families
Cyber-bullying

Internal
Workforce trends
Crime and incident reporting
Specialized units
Resources
Partnerships and partner agencies

Wicked problems

There isn't a standard format for completing a problem scan. I've seen problem scans that are the size of 'War and Peace,' though rarely actually get read by anyone. You don't need to go to that extent. It may be sufficient to take a look at a variety of topics from Box 3.2 (individually and together) and see where your local policing area compares unfavorably to the national level or to the rest of your jurisdiction. An analyst might be able to help you with this, if you have that luxury.

You can also look for problem places that have a range of negative behaviors associated with them. You could supplement this with a deeper dive into any problems with specific populations and how changes in community variables might predict emerging issues. It may be that a Compstat-type meeting flags up other issues for you to tackle. The key here is to consider the consequences for the public, and be broad in your thinking. Don't choose priorities based on numbers alone, but on the impact on the community.

Don't choose priorities based on numbers alone, but on the impact on the community.

You might have noticed one particular item in Box 3.2 is the *wicked problem*. Wicked problems are challenging social problems that are ill-formulated and may involve many decision-makers with conflicting values.[3,4] Wicked problems are places or areas where multiple factors in Box 3.2 are relevant. They are difficult to define, often unique, and have little to indicate a solution. As a leading researcher and police executive noted: "Wicked problems seldom have simple causes and usually sit across, and between different organizations or stakeholders to the point where not only is the cause and solution frequently disputed, but each apparent 'solution' often generates a further problem."[5]

Problem places can be versions of wicked problems. For example, certain bars and their immediate area can be magnets for organized crime, but also vehicle theft, drug and alcohol problems, sporadic violence, nuisance complaints, officer safety issues, and gang problems. Wicked problems are good examples of the sort of complex challenges you have likely inherited from your predecessor, chronic problems that are long-term challenges for the police. For crime problems generally, and wicked problems specifically, consider using the CHEERS framework as a way to define your problems.

THE CHEERS FRAMEWORK

Chronic problems have not been given the attention they deserve. Once a criminal family becomes embedded, or a place becomes known for street-level drug dealing or rampant disorder, it is difficult to tackle these entrenched problems. But it's not impossible. A good start is to be clear about the nature of the chronic problem. British criminologist Ron Clarke and American police researcher John Eck developed the CHEERS framework to describe and identify the key elements of a problem,[6] as shown in Box 3.3. It can be used for both chronic and spike type problems (explained in a moment). Pay particular attention to the S in CHEERS.

BOX 3.3 CHEERS ELEMENTS FOR DEFINING A PROBLEM

Community	The problems are experienced by some members of the public, such as individuals, businesses, government agencies, or other groups.
Harmful	The problem shouldn't just be against the law; it must cause harm that can involve property loss or damage, injury or death, or serious mental anguish.
Expectation	It must be evident that some members of the public expect the police to do something about the causes of the harm.
Events	There must be more than one event associated with the problem. These might be break-ins to cars, people striking each other, people exchanging money and sex, or loud motorcycles disturbing citizens.
Recurring	Having more than one event implies that events must recur. They may be symptoms of a spike or a chronic problem, but the key is that there is an expectation of continuation.
Similarity	The events must be similar or related. They may all be committed by the same person, happen to the same type of victim, occur in the same types of locations, take place in similar circumstances, involve the same type of weapon, or have one or more other factors in common.

Once you have identified a range of problems, the next stage is to determine what type of problem each is. Knowing whether a problem is a chronic issue, a recent crime spike, or a crime panic will help you better prioritize.

CHRONICS, SPIKES, AND PANICS

Many police officers think that the crime problems they face are unique; however, having spent time with cops in many countries, I've found there are many shared experiences. Chronic nuisance bars are as much of a problem in downtown San Salvador as they are in Seattle, Sydney, and Sheffield. In general, most problems seem to fall into three categories: chronic problems, crime spikes, and crime panics.

Box 3.4 lists some of the defining characteristics of these problem types. Not every problem will precisely fall into one of these categories, but you probably recognize some commonalities. Ask yourself what type of problem you are faced with, because it will help you appreciate where you need to invest time in analysis or perhaps focus on reassurance as much as crime reduction. You can see that you often get a greater sense of urgency with *panics*, yet because they are usually a long-term drain on police demand and resources, addressing *chronics* generally provides a greater return on the investment of your officers and your energy.

Chronic problems

Whenever facilitating training with police officers, I ask who has been in the same police district for at least five years. Those people are then asked to keep their hands up if there are current crime hot spots that were problems when they first started in the district. Usually every hand stays up. These are chronic problems: long-term crime problems that are often judged to be unsolvable. Street drug hot

BOX 3.4 CHRONIC, SPIKE, AND PANIC TYPES OF PROBLEMS

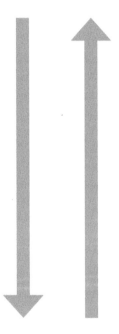

Chronics
- Ongoing sagas that have existed for months or years
- Probably inherited from previous commander
- Often blamed on social causes of crime outside of police control
- Officers frequently feel problem cannot be improved
- Skimmed over in crime management meetings

Lower sense of urgency   Higher return on investment

Spikes
- A recent and substantial increase in a problem
- Higher than expected level of crime for a place
- Identified in crime analysis as emerging crime problems
- Often a frequent topic of crime management meetings

Panics
- Similar to a spike but may not have a significant increase in crime frequency
- Perceived as having a disproportionate impact on crime fear
- May be generated by political or media attention
- Can be associated with a moral panic
- Frequently one of the first topics in crime management meetings

Greater sense of urgency   Lower return on investment

spots, areas with multigenerational crime families, and gang areas often fall into this category.

> *Pessimism often pervades the discussion around chronic problems, because of a sense that 'everything has been done and nothing works.' This quickly migrates to being 'nothing can be done.'*

Chronic problems are often persistent challenges, yet can be ignored or written off by many people as 'just the way things are.' They become an accepted part of the landscape, among both the public and the police. But this acceptance doesn't detract from the reality that they are a constant irritant. Pessimism often pervades the discussion around chronic problems, because of a sense that 'everything has been done and nothing works.' This quickly migrates to being 'nothing can be done.' 'Nothing can be done' is code for 'none of our traditional responses work.' Often, however, the problem has not been examined with a fresh perspective that focuses on precise data analysis and an intelligence-led intervention.

A good commander will always be working on at least one chronic problem, and makes chronic problems the priority.

Crime spikes

Almost the opposite of chronic problems, crime spikes are frequently fascinating to executive leadership because they provide some relief from the repetitive monotony of fretting over the chronic problems. As a result, police chiefs love discussing spikes in crime management meetings. A crime spike is a sudden and often surprising increase in, or appearance of, a crime problem. Tackling emerging crime problems can be important, but they can too often take precedence over chronic problems. Also, because they are new and emerging, there is sometimes a rush to action before the crime spike is fully understood (Box 3.5).

BOX 3.5 CHALLENGING A CRIME SPIKE FOCUS

"Our leadership are great, though sometimes they get a little overly fixated with crime spikes while ignoring the long-term challenges that have been in the district for years. Yet if they could make a dent in those, it would improve their numbers to a far greater extent than rushing to address a spike that might not be a big deal anyway. Focusing on crime spikes results in a 'whack-a-mole' approach to policing. It would generally be more productive to focus on repeats and multi-repeats such as offenders, victims and locations which often overlap, as these are often predictable and frequently in locations that they are expected to happen."

Neil Trainor is a supervisor in a New Zealand Police intelligence unit currently supervising the Tamaki Makaurau robbery intelligence team.

Spikes in crime and disorder will garner attention because of their novelty. I've seen this in the management gatherings of many agencies. In one Florida sheriff's department, a map showed a multitude of dots that were crying out for action, but they were in the usual place. Everyone had grown accustomed to these. I could quickly determine that the entire room was bored by them. So, the focus instead turned to a much smaller cluster of a few new dots in an unexpected place, and the meeting ended up dominated by this minor blip. It was like Dug the dog in the Pixar animated movie *Up*, who gets easily distracted by a "squirrel!" Everyone seemed relieved to have a chance to demonstrate their leadership and act decisively on an emerging issue rather than refocus back onto the much bigger, but more intractable problem.

This is the crime spike bias. Crime spike bias happens when chronic issues are relegated in favor of emerging crime problems that are actually less harmful. Acting quickly and decisively is often seen as demonstrative of strong leadership in policing. But, in the absence of good evaluation, the frequent failure that results from rushing to a poor decision is rarely discovered. People get quickly caught up in the next drama.

Too many people get overexcited about crime spikes that are often just the predictable result of seasonality. This is the regular change in crime rates for some offenses that can be attributed to seasonal changes in weather and hours of daylight. For example, violence can increase in the summer as people spend more time outside socializing and interacting with other citizens. Across the United States, summer burglary rates are about 10 percent higher than in winter.[7] And, as you can see in Figure 3.2, pickpocketing and associated property losses spike spectacularly every year during the annual Mardi Gras festival in the U.S. city of New Orleans. This event brings over a million revelers to the 8th police district, centered on the famous French Quarter. It also brings thieves.

Monthly count in New Orleans' 8th District

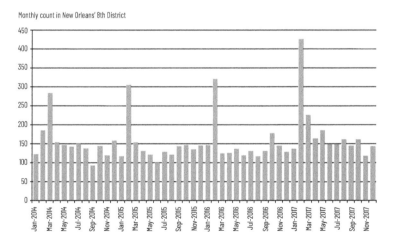

Figure 3.2 Pickpocketing and asociated property loss in New Orleans 8th Police District

Crime spikes can also be resolved by (or vulnerable to) regression to the mean (Box 3.6). That being said, if a crime spike is an emerging problem, trying to address it in its relative infancy can be useful before it gains a foothold and becomes an established (and chronic) concern.

> Acting quickly and decisively is often seen as demonstrative of strong leadership in policing, but in the absence of good evaluation, the frequent failure that results from rushing a poor decision is rarely discovered.

While you might be under pressure to make a snap decision, try and use the PANDA model and ideas in this book to implement a more thoughtful, long-term approach to the problem.

Crime panics

Crime panics are problems that might be crime spikes (in that they may be concerning increases in crime). More often, they may be driven by media and political concern as much as a genuine emergence of a crime problem. In the U.K., these can be referred to as signal crimes, because they disproportionately affect the public's belief or behavior regarding their perception of risk.[8] They sometimes revolve around moral panics (like sexual assaults or crimes against children) that are fortunately infrequent yet still dramatically skew the public's sense of risk and concern. You know a moral panic is circulating when the press starting using words like 'evil' and 'horror.' While crime spikes might garner attention, crime panics definitely will.

This isn't to negate the impact of a horrible crime on the immediate victims; but, as we have often seen, a single rare and unusual event can impact the risk perceptions of people hundreds of miles away. A grizzly murder can fill the news cycle for days, yet the homicide risk for most people doesn't change. The media's fascination with murder seems misplaced until you understand that their priority is selling advertising and newspapers. Terrible crimes sell tabloids. Panics can even occur because journalists misinterpret data or don't understand seasonality. So, don't assume that a recent crime panic is indicative that a significant problem is emerging, at least until regression to the mean is ruled out. Regression to the mean is sometimes referred to as the Sports Illustrated jinx, as explained in Box 3.6.

BOX 3.6 THE SPORTS ILLUSTRATED JINX

Random fluctuation of a crime rate is normal. Crime isn't completely predictable because changes in many things such as the weather or even an important sports game on the television can affect the availability of offenders and potential crime victims. Unfortunately, this normal fluctuation can be mistaken as a spike. Police can expend considerable effort dealing with a crime spike that, if left unattended, would likely return back to the normal level of crime after a short while. Statisticians now call this regression to the mean, though when first described it was (fittingly) called regression to mediocrity by English statistician, Sir Francis Galton. It is analogous to what is sometimes called the Sports Illustrated jinx.

Sports Illustrated is a magazine that often features on the cover athletes or teams who have been recently successful and who have lately been winning more games than normal. They then become victims of the Sports Illustrated jinx by having a poor spell after appearing on the magazine cover. Rather than being a victim of a jinx, the athletes are simply regressing to their average (known as the mean) performance level. Sports stars and teams tend to have good and bad games, but not in a regular pattern. They have good and bad streaks. After a good run, they tend to return to their normal performance level as the good and bad games even themselves out over time. This can often also be the case with crime levels.

Chronics, spikes, and panics

No doubt there are some crimes and crime series that do not fit neatly into one of the three categories, but on the whole these classifications cover much of what you will have to deal with. Giving thought to what type of problem you have will help with the remainder of PANDA. Because these problems have—at least to management—an increasing sense of urgency (see arrow in Box 3.4), each problem type may require a different approach in the later stages of PANDA.

In your analysis phase, chronic problems have usually survived extensive attempts to resolve them and will need a thorough and careful analysis if you are to be effective. When you deploy your solution (D in PANDA), chronic problems may require more assistance from partnership agencies outside of law enforcement so you can achieve cost-effective, long-term reductions.

Crime spikes may instead need a quicker and more responsive law enforcement response than you might design for a chronic problem, and a crime panic might require you to place more focus on reassurance policing. Panics may also require a rapid analysis to establish the real extent of the problem and a response that can alleviate the political or media pressure.

AN EXAMPLE PROBLEM SCAN

While the problem scan can raise your awareness of problems you might want to target, it is not designed to give you an in-depth understanding of each problem you face. That is the purpose of the A in PANDA, which we will get to in the next chapter. At this stage, a suitable course of action is to draw up a chart of all the problems you have identified, and classify them into chronic, spike or panic. Once you have done that, determine a draft prioritization order for tackling them. You probably can't decide yet how many you can tackle, because that is a resource issue. But, for now, you should at least have a list of priorities, what type of problem they are, and a rough estimate of where they are in order of importance. Senior officers or colleagues can also provide some input to your priority list.

Let's use the example of Amy, a new area commander in a suburban district, who arrived at the district in the last month. In that time, she has attended a Compstat meeting, a community meeting, and has been emailed numerous times by the mayor's office. She is starting to gather a list of the problems she is expected to address. Amy puts the list on a whiteboard and categorizes them by their problem type (chronic, spike, or panic). She also notes the source and has a first pass at a priority order based on an estimate of both the quantity and harm of the problems (Table 3.1).

Amy limits herself to only a couple of priority one problems, so that her limited resources and energies are not stretched too far. She also notes that she will need to follow up with the crime analysis team at headquarters, or invest some of her own time, to better understand the panics. Crime analysis will tell her whether the theft from cars near the housing project is more than just a panic, and she can ask a community support officer to ask the elementary school more about the graffiti problem that was flagged up by the Mayor's office. With

Table 3.1 Example list of problems and their classification

Problem	Source	Type	Priority
Residential burglary in housing project	Crime analysis	Chronic	1
Thefts from cars near supermarket	Crime analysis	Chronic	2
Traffic congestion around Saturday street market	Compstat meeting	Chronic	3
Speeding cars outside high school	Community meeting	Spike	3
Thefts from cars near the housing project	Community meeting	Panic	2
Gang graffiti near the elementary school	Mayor's office	Panic	2
Rowdy youths causing disturbances near community center	Mayor's office	Chronic	3
Noisy late night crowds outside Willie's bar and neighboring establishments	Community meeting	Chronic	2
Increase in assault complaints at Willie's bar	Crime analysis	Spike	1

her list intact, she can then discuss her priorities moving forward with the police chief at their next meeting. She can go to Compstat armed with a much better understanding of the range and scope of the issues she has to address.

CHAPTER SUMMARY

- Senior commanders appreciate the view from 30,000 feet.
- At the local area level, step back and think about your local policing area from 'pattern altitude.'
- From an area commander's perspective, pattern altitude allows you to assess the local context of your area problems and compare them to city-wide issues.
- Consider the social harms of criminality and disorder as well as crime.
- Use the CHEERS framework as part of your problem scan.
- Classify each problem as chronic, spike, or panic.
- Be alert for regression to the mean with spikes and panics that might dissipate without needing action.
- Be aware that seasonality is a factor for many crime problems.
- List your area's problems and classification (chronic, spike, panic), and determine a draft priority order.
- Try and maintain a focus on at least one chronic problem.

REFERENCES

1 Ratcliffe, J.H., *Intelligence-Led Policing* (2nd edition). 2016, Abingdon, Oxon.: Routledge.
2 Ratcliffe, J.H., *Towards an index for harm-focused policing.* Policing: A Journal of Policy and Practice, 2015. **9**(2): p. 164–82.
3 Churchman, C.W., *Wicked problems.* Management Science, 1967. **14**(4): p. 141–42.
4 Rittel, H.W.J. and M.M. Webber, *Dilemmas in a general theory of planning.* Policy Sciences, 1973. **4**(2): p. 155–69.

5   Grint, K. and S. Thornton, *Leadership, management, and command in the police* in *Police Leadership: Rising to the Top*, J. Fleming, Editor. 2015, Oxford: Oxford University Press. p. 95–109.

6   Clarke, R.V. and J. Eck, *Crime analysis for problem solvers: In 60 small steps*. 2005, Washington, D.C.: Center for Problem Oriented Policing.

7   Lauritsen, J.L. and N. White, *Seasonal patterns in criminal victimization trends*. 2014, Bureau of Justice Statistics: Washington, D.C. p. 21.

8   Innes, M., *Reinventing tradition? Reassurance, neighbourhood security and policing*. Criminal Justice, 2004. **4**(2): p. 151–71.

4

ANALYZING CRIME PROBLEMS

WHY ANALYSIS IS VITAL TO REDUCING CRIME

Foot patrol in the middle of a winter's night isn't exactly a sought-after assignment, and this night was particularly chilly. I was starting to lose the feeling in my toes. My colleague and I whiled away our time staring in the windows of the closed shops of the Roman Road Market in London's East End. There was little else to do at four o'clock in the morning. The market area had a vehicle theft problem, and we had been assigned to an intensive foot patrol. There wasn't a soul on the street.

I was aware that the market had a vehicle crime problem because earlier that week I had spoken to the collator, the genial officer who ran the intelligence office at Bow Road police station. He mainly kept the criminal histories of known offenders updated. Index cards were removed from the wall of cases that stretched across the expansive office, and new information was typed by hand onto the next space on the card. Prolific offenders with long criminal histories would have a plastic sheath to hold all of their cards together. Responding to my query about the Roman Road assignment, the collator looked up from his antiquated typewriter and lamented: "The stall holders are always getting stuff nicked, and people coming to the market leave things in their cars, no matter how often we tell them not to. Oh yeah," he continued, "market days are always busy for car break-ins."

The market operated during the day on Tuesdays, Thursdays, and Saturdays, so why was I risking frostbite at 4am on a Monday morning? It might be that my area commander genuinely thought that a night-time foot patrol seven days a week was appropriate. Or he wanted to placate the community. Or he knew it was a fruitless exercise but still had to reassure a senior officer that 'something was being done about the problem.'

But it might also have been that the commander had not gathered sufficient information to really understand the problem. Nobody had been assigned to scrutinize the crime reports, speak to the collator, or study the problem in any depth.

> Reflective practice isn't exactly respected in a policing profession that venerates quick, decisive action.

The first A in PANDA is for *Analyze* (or *Analyze* problem). Most people would agree that some analysis of a problem is a precursor to making a good decision, but few actually think about the *process* of analysis. And in the heat of pressure from the media or in a crime management meeting like Compstat, some commanders abandon any sense of process and start winging it. In the hot seat, they rush to their comfortable, decision-making role. Reflective practice isn't exactly respected in a policing profession that venerates quick, decisive action.

In the end, we too often grasp at any solution that we have heard about, judge might work, or is what we did last time. As former CIA analysis chief Morgan Jones has said: "The crushing necessity to make the problem 'go away now' makes us receptive to *any* solution that will provide even temporary relief from an oppressive situation."[1] Cognitive psychologists are very clear that unstructured analysis is inefficient and error prone. Jones suggests that intuitive, amorphous thinking can lead to a number of problems, including:

- beginning analysis by forming conclusions
- focusing on the solution we intuitively prefer
- settling for the first solution that appears satisfactory
- considering discussing or thinking hard about a problem as being the same as analyzing it
- focusing on the substance rather than the process of analysis.

By relying on our intuition, we also tend to be closed to other options or perceive cause and effect and links where none exist. When the media or public do this, crime panics can result.

The solution is a more structured analytical process. Whether you do the analysis yourself or whether you have the luxury of tasking a crime analyst, there are ways you can structure the analytical process that will improve your outcomes. Tasking (either of yourself or someone else, such as an analyst) involves setting an appropriate analytical question related to an outcome you want to influence. When you do this for yourself or a crime analyst, use some of the ideas described later in Table 4.1 to set questions that will generate more illuminating answers.

You can also structure an exploratory analysis around the VOLTAGE checklist. This framework is designed not only to identify what you know about a crime problem, but also to identify areas where your knowledge may be weaker. It forces you to think about different aspects of the problem, and in doing so perhaps identify possible avenues you had not previously considered.

VOLTAGE

Whether you have a chronic crime problem, a spike, or a panic (see Chapter 3), the *Analyze* stage of PANDA has a number of different pieces you should consider. One is to appreciate what you know and what you don't know. You could wrap yourself up in analysis, endlessly diving down a Donald Rumsfeldian rabbit hole of 'unknown unknowns' (see Box 4.1), but this can lead to paralysis-by-analysis. Instead, use the VOLTAGE checklist as a structured approach that makes sure you have at least covered some of the basic components necessary to make an informed decision. VOLTAGE is an extension of a simple analytical tool (VOLT) that has previously been used in some police services as a framework for structuring knowledge about crime problems.[2] It is connected to the crime triangle that you will learn about in the next chapter.

With chronic problems you should definitely invest effort in establishing what you know and want to know in the VOLTAGE

BOX 4.1 "THERE ARE ALSO UNKNOWN UNKNOWNS"

In 2002, then U.S. Secretary of Defense Donald Rumsfeld gave a response to a question about the absence of evidence linking Iraq with weapons of mass destruction. In doing so, he achieved some fleeting notoriety for his rather tortured phrasing:

> "Reports that say that something hasn't happened are always interesting to me, because as we know, there are known knowns; there are things we know we know. We also know there are known unknowns; that is to say we know there are some things we do not know. But there are also unknown unknowns – the ones we don't know we don't know. And if one looks throughout the history of our country and other free countries, it is the latter category that tend to be the difficult ones."

With his 'unknown unknowns', Rumsfeld was talking about the challenge of identifying risks or factors that are so unusual that they wouldn't normally occur to us. The VOLTAGE checklist is designed to give you a list of considerations in respect to a crime problem. It should help you confirm what you know (your 'known knowns'), identify what would be useful to your decision-making but that you don't know (your 'known unknowns'), and perhaps open up the possibility of considering knowledge you didn't even appreciate might be available or needed (your 'unknown unknowns').

framework. With crime spikes you may be under pressure to respond quickly, but at least some cursory attention to addressing the VOLTAGE framework may help you find a better initial response. You can then use your response to gather more information and fill intelligence gaps in VOLTAGE.

For example, saturation patrols may help alleviate a short-term problem, but they can also forage information that will inform a subsequent long-term plan. You can task them to report back to you or an analyst. You can even go further, as Kelly Robbins explains later in Box 4.6.

Be aware that crime panics may or may not evolve into long-term problems. Attention to the TIMES component* (T in VOLTAGE) may be useful in placing the current panic into more historical context. Has it been a seasonal problem every year, or is it currently no higher than it has been in the past? The media often return to old stories to update their audience, regardless of whether there is a new problem. Don't forget that the primary aim of newspapers is not to proportionately and accurately reflect local crime concerns on your behalf. The VOLTAGE components are shown in Box 4.2 along with some example questions.

BOX 4.2 VOLTAGE FRAMEWORK FOR ANALYZING CRIME PROBLEMS

Component	Example questions to answer
Victims	Does crime concentrate among a certain type of victim or target? Are there multiple victims or is a particular target the subject of repeat victimization? Does the type of target generate particular public concern (such as children)?
Offenders	Is the crime problem created by numerous offenders who are not known to each other? Is it caused by a few repeat offenders? Are there new offenders in the area (prison releases)?

Locations	Are specific places targeted, or is crime distributed more widely? What is special about the place? Is it a particular location (such as a bar), a particular street (with a troublesome family), or an area (housing project or nighttime economy zone)?
Times	Is the crime problem within normal variation or explainable by annual seasonal patterns? If not, are there specific times when crime is concentrated? Are new patterns evident?
Attractors	Are particular locations or places attracting offenders because of the easy criminal opportunities (attractors) or are places inadvertently creating crime opportunities (generators)? Where are the worst places?
Groups	Are gangs or inter-gang conflicts a factor? Is organized crime involved? Are school children involved either as offenders or victims? Are there disputes between criminal families, or fans of particular sports teams?
Enhancers	Are factors such as drug or alcohol use a factor to consider? Are behavioral (mental) health issues part of the problem?

Reviewing what is known about a crime problem through a structure such as VOLTAGE can also reveal what is not known. These unknowns can become important intelligence gaps to address in your tactical response.

CRIME ANALYSIS

To populate your VOLTAGE framework, focus on three main sources. Most police information comes from the three Cs of crime analysis, criminal intelligence, and community information.

Crime analysis has emerged as a significant discipline within law enforcement over the last 30 years. It has grown as interest in data-driven approaches to policing have become possible. Some police services have dedicated analytical staff, while smaller departments may have sworn officers who also double as an analyst. If you are in a small agency, or at a remote location, you might have to be your own analyst.

Most police information comes from the three Cs of crime analysis, criminal intelligence, and community information.

Crime analysis might not be the most accurate term. Analysts can often spend their time exploring events that are not strictly crimes. There is significant value in understanding and preventing noise problems, patterns of domestic disputes, panhandling, and traffic accidents. A good analyst can help you go beyond a basic description of *what* and get deeper into the causality of *why*. They can be worth their weight in gold (see Box 5.6 in the next chapter).

The secret to good analysis is to develop *good questions, good data,* and *good thinking. Good questions* move beyond just describing a problem. How many burglaries did we have this month compared to last month is a descriptive question. You can ask that of a crime analyst, or even research it yourself, but it doesn't tell you anything about *why.* Questions that start with *why* often elicit more insightful responses. For example, asking 'why are burglaries clustered in one place?' might need more time to study and even development of different data sources, but it is a question that will generate a useful answer. Table 4.1 shows other good questions that can help you move beyond just descriptive responses. If you are in a senior leadership position, these questions are also good to ask in Compstat meetings.

Table 4.1 Analytical framing questions and examples

Aim	Bad question	Better question	Why it is a better question
Ask questions that challenge assumptions	"The chief says burglaries have increased significantly in our district... What are we going to do about it?"	"Have burglaries increased significantly in our district as the police chief thinks?"	The better question does not assume that the chief is right, but instead checks what the data say. The answer might avoid an unnecessary crime panic.
Try and ask a why question	"How much have burglaries increased in the last month?"	"Why have burglaries increased in the last month?"	A why question will give you a greater chance of understanding the drivers behind the problem.
Don't build assumptions into the question	"We need to show that the 456 gang are responsible for the increase in burglaries."	"Is there a relationship between local gangs and burglaries?"	Doesn't assume that the gangs are responsible, but leaves that as a possibility for the data to show.
Don't tie tactics to questions	"Where should I deploy uniform foot patrols to reduce street robberies?"	"How can I best address street robberies?"	Doesn't tie you into a specific tactic before you've done any analysis.
Avoid vague or overly broad questions	"What should we do about all the violence in this district?"	"Where and when is street violence concentrated?" or "what are our domestic violence patterns?"	A specific question about where and when is a starting point to more focused policing answers.
Avoid questions that suggest a pre-determined response	"Burglaries have increased. How can we arrest more burglars?"	"Why are burglaries increasing?" or "How can we prevent burglaries from continuing to increase?"	Avoids a pre-determined response or tactical reaction that may skew the analysis and draw away from more imaginative solutions.

Good data should be fit for your purpose. In other words, the data you base decisions on should be *accurate, precise, consistent, complete,* and *reliable.*[3] Accuracy and precision are necessary for local analysis. For example, it will be difficult to identify repeat victimization of an individual address if your officers only record crime locations as the nearest street intersection or as a street block. Consistency and reliability are important for the T (times) in VOLTAGE. If your agency changes the criteria for what counts as an attempted crime, this can make it difficult to look at historical patterns and determine if you have a crime spike. Completeness is the last component. I once worked with a police department that was unable to map any crime that occurred in a new housing project. Rather than rectify the situation, they seemed happy that there was a large area of their city that appeared to have no crime. The command staff seemed oblivious to the fact that only about 70 percent of their violent crime was on the map.

If, as a police leader, you accept poor report writing in your officers, then you will forever be vulnerable to the garbage-in-garbage-out problem. I consulted with a Sheriff's department in Florida where the major in charge of patrol acknowledged they never bothered to analyze data related to modus operandi, because, as he said, "We know the deputies never record that correctly." He just shrugged his shoulders and figured his deputies were never going to fill the report field properly. It never occurred to him to have his colleagues better supervise their deputies.

Good thinking means having an open mind. This means avoiding confirmation bias. This is a cognitive failure that results in our tendency to search for or interpret information in such a way that it confirms our preconceived ideas about a situation. I've watched police executives ask analysts to gather data that "shows our operation was a success" or "look at the offenders in this area because the 456 gang are responsible for the recent shootings." Confirmation bias happens when we seek out information, or give more weight to data, that confirms what we already suspect or want to believe. It's a common pitfall. By not being open to different possibilities, we can get locked into a loop of perpetually failing to solve a problem or appreciate a different perspective. You might have noticed this with colleagues who blindly follow a certain political ideology and are unable to appreciate alternative viewpoints.

The VOLTAGE checklist is designed to promote good thinking by encouraging you to see the problem from different perspectives and not focus on one cause. If used properly, this can prevent you assuming that the problem is just caused by particular offenders (O in VOLTAGE) or the behavior of particular victims (V in VOLTAGE).

CRIMINAL INTELLIGENCE

As stated in the previous section, good crime analysis will tell you what is going on. But it might not tell you why. That's where criminal intelligence enters the fray.

Quality intelligence on gangs and organized crime groups rarely comes from community meetings or the local minister. It comes from an offender's disgruntled neighbors, jilted lovers, and cheated co-offenders. One afternoon at the front office of Bow Road police station, a woman strode up to the counter, looked me straight in the eye, and said: "My husband is a drug dealer and a cheating son-of-a-bitch. I want to tell you everything that he's been doing."

> Natural police seems to involve officers who display a combination of intelligence, curiosity, empathy, tenacity, and related policing skills.

Quality informants rarely present themselves so handily! Good criminal intelligence generally comes through officers who have a connection with the street. They have what we used to call a "good copper's nose," cops who can establish a rapport with offenders and from there develop informants. One Philadelphia cop, Shawn Hagan, told me that a sense of empathy is important when dealing with active criminals. He argued that an appreciation for what forces have operated on their lives helped him realize that things aren't always black and white, or good and evil. On a drive around his district in Philadelphia, he once said to me: "If you grow up here, go to these schools, and hang around these corners, of course you will likely end up in a gang. What else is there to do here?" Shawn wasn't excusing criminal behavior or suggesting that serious crime shouldn't be punished. Far from it. It was more mitigation, an acknowledgment of an offender's guilt while understanding at least some of the structural forces that might have propelled them there.

Policing is full of real-life examples of a Sam Vimes (the marvelous fictional policemen from Terry Pratchett's Discworld book series) or a Lester Freamon (the smart and insightful detective from the HBO series *The Wire*). In other words, people who are—to use a term from *The Wire*—'natural police.' Natural police seems to involve officers who display a combination of intelligence, curiosity, empathy, tenacity, and related policing skills. My first exposure to 'natural police' was a former sergeant of mine, Phil Gospage, who had an uncanny knack of connecting with offenders in a way that they respected. He understood their motivations and needs. People cooperate with the police for many different reasons, so this empathy is important in understanding an informant's motivation. After all, you can't develop a contact if you don't understand what they want or need. They may come to you in search of leniency or out of an altruistic sense of community pride. Be prepared to be flexible and work with the informant's needs as much as your own.

Since my time working with Phil Gospage in the east end of London, I've met 'natural police' in just about every department I've worked. These are the officers that are often respected by their peers. Their status as 'natural police' transcends rank. It is assigned by colleagues and earned with a capacity that is neither easy to learn nor evaluate with an examination. It is part of the craft of policing. Natural police can be particularly adept at recruiting informants (see Box 4.3 and later Box 8.3).

BOX 4.3 RECRUITING CONFIDENTIAL HUMAN INFORMATION SOURCES (INFORMANTS)

According to the International Association of Chiefs of Police, *general sources* are other law enforcement officers or officials; *citizen sources* are crime victims, witnesses, and other concerned citizens; and *street sources* are people who come into contact with police because of their occupations, activities, or where they live. The most challenging is the *confidential informant*, "an individual, who, in an arrangement with law enforcement authorities, agrees to serve in a clandestine capacity to gather information for those authorities on suspected criminal activity or known criminal operatives in exchange for compensation or consideration."[4]

The criminally-involved confidential informant seeking financial reward or leniency can be problematic, but also be hugely useful. As one homicide detective said, "If all we ever use are altar boys, all we will ever catch are priests."[5]

Frequently, informants are recruited through being asked to cooperate after formally recorded interviews.[6] An old friend, who spent years as a detective inspector in North London, had many recruitment successes by reaching out to non-crime associates and family of gang members. These disgruntled girlfriends or parents who wanted an intervention could provide significant insight into criminal gangs.

Little research exists on the particular skills of good recruiters; however, you might seek officers who easily engage in conversation with the public, get out of the patrol car to talk to people, have an ease with offenders and never display hostility or contempt for them. A little dignity and respect goes a long way. Empathy, resilience, humility, good communication and listening skills, and an awareness of body language are also useful.

Handling of potential sources from the criminal world should only be done after suitable training in your department's procedures and all appropriate legislation, and a grounding in operational objectives and limits.

Tapping into this rich vein of knowledge can be a challenge. Criminal intelligence, while often full of meaning, is often unstructured in nature. It can be relatively random without a sense of context, and officers may not know that you need it. Without being aware of your needs, it often stays locked up inside their heads. Good intelligence can be gathered by a criminal intelligence unit (if you have one), and you should check with them. But this assumes that your 'natural police' are communicating with the intelligence unit, that the unit is recording and classifying the information, and, finally, that the unit can recall and deliver the intelligence to you in a timely manner.

It is important to get a feel for who is 'natural police' (see Box 4.4) and who is a Walt Disney. Shawn Hagan gets credit for this one. Walt Disneys are police officers who—while well-meaning—think they

---

BOX 4.4 CHIEF CONSTABLE WENSLEY ON 'NATURAL POLICE'

A century ago, Chief Constable Wensley of the Criminal Investigation Department of Scotland Yard was aware of the value of 'natural police,' writing in 1931:[?]

"In truth, all the mechanical ingenuity in the world will never stamp the criminal out. The only real method is to employ detectives who *know* rogues by direct contact, know their habits, their ways of thought, their motives, and above all, know their friends and associates. In the vast majority of cases information can only be gained in this way.

For a large part of my life I was thrown into close contact with some of the most desperate rogues in London. I have eaten with them, drunk with them, and mixed with them in every variety of circumstance. . . . Criminals, I early found, were human beings, and enthusiastic though I was, I never allowed myself to hunt them with any violent bitterness. I always tried to keep a perspective. As a professional crook once said to me, after I had laid hands on him, 'If it wasn't for the like of us the like of you wouldn't be wanted.'"

know what is happening on the street, but don't have as much insight as they think. A Walt Disney will tell you a good story, but it is largely a fairytale. As a commander, if you want to cultivate 'natural police' then find a way to reward good information and create a process to bring you this knowledge.

A final note on working with a crime analyst or good intelligence officer. If you are lucky enough to have access to these resources, you should consider their role. The 3-i intelligence-led policing model explains that the role of the analyst is not just to *interpret* (the first i) the criminal environment, but also to *influence* (the second i) the thinking of a decision-maker, who in turn has an *impact* (the last i) on the criminal environment.[2] A more recent iteration adds a fourth 'i,' which you can see in Figure 4.1.

As a commander, you have two responsibilities in the relationship. You should keep the analyst or intelligence officer informed as to your *intent*. What are the problems that are important to you, and what are likely future concerns? Second, a commander has a duty to allow the analyst to *influence* their thinking so that analysis and criminal intelligence can help have an impact on the criminal environment.

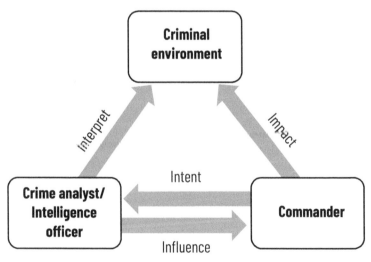

Figure 4.1 The 4-i model of intelligence-led policing

This requires you, as a commander, to do a few simple things when lucky enough to have access to a crime analyst or intelligence officer (the specific organizational terms are unimportant and generally refer to anyone who has an analytical capacity that can help you). They are:

1 Keep the analyst regularly updated and informed about your priorities and concerns. They are not mind-readers, and can't guess what crime issues you want to focus on.
2 Create a process where you can be influenced by, and learn from, the analyst. This means being open-minded and willing to encourage imagination and different possibilities. It is more than just reading reports sent to you, but instead actively engaging with the analyst as a partner in the analysis. Give them a seat at the big table.
3 Be willing to use analytical reports as part of your VOLTAGE process and incorporate them into your final strategic plan. Analysts and police officers will lose faith in you quickly if you receive briefings that indicate a changing criminal environment but you do not change your strategy accordingly.

COMMUNITY INFORMATION

While many police departments talk about community policing, it has long been recognized that agencies haven't done a great job of incorporating community information and concerns into their decision-making.[8] The community meeting has long been the staple of police-community relations; however, there are three general concerns with these events.

First, it is often unclear what the purpose of the meeting is. In some places it is a way to tell the community what the police have been doing. In others a forum for the community to help the police choose priorities. In yet others a mechanism for people to report crime and issues. In some jurisdictions it is an unstructured mish-mash. Second, because only certain groups attend community gatherings, they can hijack the priorities. The community is not served when the meetings are commandeered by one segment of the population. Finally, the meetings (like Compstat sessions) can become rote and ritualized, finishing exactly on time once everyone has gone through the motions.

But before you write them off, ponder the crime funnel later in Figure 6.1 on page 102. For every 1,000 crimes and disorder issues experienced by the public, police data systems only record about 429. We miss a great deal of information if we don't have direct neighborhood contact. Community meetings can be a valuable information gathering tool, as long as the meeting has clear objectives, as Martin Gallagher explains in Box 4.5.

BOX 4.5 A FOCUSED APPROACH TO COMMUNITY PARTNERSHIP MEETINGS

"When I arrived in Paisley as the area commander I had never worked there before. The division had stressed enforcement and moved away from community outreach. I attended partnership meetings but it was clear that we were missing a good degree of community penetration. There was no real forum for community leaders to meet and talk and there were no processes or goals evident. I identified that we needed to first establish a *temperature gauge* for community sentiment, and second develop, when temperaments were cool, a relationship we could lean on if things were about to boil over.

Over the next four months I met with various groups and individuals, such as the local bishop, imam, and minority communities. We formed the 'Grey Space Group,' which now has over 20 members. We meet quarterly and I report crime trends and in-depth updates on specific hate crimes. Then we discuss community issues, contentious media reporting, and changes in the wider world that might affect Paisley. This has resulted in a lot of useful intelligence, largely gathered through established trust. We are now developing how to leverage the group in supporting statutory agencies if we encounter any future crisis events. This all grew from being clear about what we were missing and what we wanted the forum to achieve."

Martin Gallagher is currently a chief inspector in Police Scotland assigned as area commander in Paisley (U.K.).

One way to partially fill the gap is with regular community surveys, as recommended by the President's Task Force on 21st Century Policing.[9] Too few police departments conduct systematic and organized surveys of their communities, which makes somewhat of a mockery of their claims regarding community policing.

There are few standard surveys, though the National Police Research Platform (nationalpoliceresearch.org) has a number of downloadable surveys and reports available to members. If your own police force doesn't have a survey, you can design and distribute your own. A local academic institution might be able to help you, and you could ask community officers to distribute it. I have placed a version of a survey that I used with the Philadelphia Police Department on the website that supports this book. Surveys cannot be *ad hoc*, one-off affairs, but instead should be done regularly so you can see what has changed from one time period to another. Focus on perceived crime problems and perceptions of police. Smaller-scale surveys can also be useful to help you understand the dimensions of a specific problem (see Box 4.6).

Another source of community information that is more problem-specific is to task your officers to tap into street sources (see Box 4.3). These are people who come into contact with police because of their occupations, activities, or where they live. They include bar employees, doormen, cab drivers, workers in convenience stores, and even prostitutes. Many of them will have a vested interest in keeping crime low. In some cases, they are place managers (see Chapter 5), who while not formally employed in a crime prevention role can help in terms of informal surveillance and exercise some crime limiting effect. Even if people are on the fringes of society and sometimes benefit from crime, they may be vehemently opposed to more serious offending. For example, homeless people and prostitutes are often concerned about violence directed towards their communities. Fremont (California) Police Department has an officer who works closely with their homeless population, tapping into their knowledge about the local area. Adam Foster is affectionately known as 'the homeless whisperer.'

BOX 4.6 UNDERSTANDING A BURGLARY PROBLEM WITH SURVEYS

"In Philadelphia's 25th district, known as the Badlands, most officers can consider themselves veterans of the policing profession within one year. Crime is diverse and unrelenting. When I began to analyze residential burglaries in the district, I had five years under my belt and was a member of our proactive patrol team. We were expected to know our major crime patterns, main 'doers,' and active warrants. I considered myself a salty old district expert who knew far more about the burglary patterns than any analysis could ever tell me. After studying burglary reports in a structured way, I was surprised by the results: they were completely different from my original beliefs. I asked foot patrol officers to do a survey of burglary victims. While they grumbled quite a bit, I was supported by my captain and the results reinforced our new insight.

The surveys confirmed that my preconceptions about the problem needed adjusting. Burglaries were committed in broad daylight with no subterfuge, by kicking in the front or back door. Offenders lived nearby and stole electronics that were difficult to conceal under a jacket or in a backpack. This put a whole new perspective on our burglary problem. Our community approach to remind residents to lock their doors was completely ineffective. Most of the residences surveyed had bolt locks on their doors and homeowners routinely locked them. But the offenders knew the area, were blatantly kicking in doors, and didn't mind being seen walking down the street with visible electronics. This insight changed our entire approach."

Kelly Robbins is currently a sergeant in the Philadelphia Police Department, Pennsylvania (U.S.) where she is assigned to a regional operations command.

A BURGLARY EXAMPLE

If you recall, Amy is our local area commander at a suburban district. At the recent management meeting, the police chief looked at the map and said, "Your burglaries have gone through the roof. What's going on?" Before she could answer, the head of detectives jumps in with: "It's that MS-13 gang. I went to a briefing from the local counter-terrorism center and they said these gangs would soon be spreading from the city to our entire region."

The police chief responds: "The Mayor's next door neighbor was broken into during the middle of the night. She doesn't live in your area, but there is clearly a problem with nighttime burglaries in our town." The deputy chief feels like he has to say something, so chips in with: "The district across town has been plagued by louts coming from the city at the weekends causing all kinds of havoc. I'll bet they are responsible." Smartly, Amy defers and requests some time to do an analysis of the problem.

Amy appears to have an emerging burglary spike so sets about completing a VOLTAGE analysis. A crime analyst at headquarters charts her burglaries over the last couple of years and confirms there is a growing problem that isn't due to seasonality. The analyst also tells Amy that most of the burglaries take place during the day in the middle of the week, when many crime victims are at work (T in VOLTAGE). A number of locations have been burgled more than once, indicative of repeat victimization (V in VOLTAGE). One housing project in particular has been heavily targeted, often at the rear of the houses through patio doors (L), though the crime reports are not always completed properly so this is difficult to confirm. The patrol teams have only made one arrest for burglary recently, and that was of a local youth who stole items to fuel his heroin addiction (O). Little is known about offenders otherwise.

Amy telephones a local detective known to be good 'natural police.' Jim tells Amy that on the street they are seeing a new type of heroin mixed with fentanyl that is attracting drug users from outside the area (E and O). One of the local neighborhood gangs might be taking property in lieu of cash for drug purchases (G) and have been sending drug users out to burgle from the older residents of the housing project (G). While the drug connection is interesting, Jim's hunch is that local kids are playing truant and have started breaking into houses when they know home owners are away (O and V).

In a team meeting, one of Amy's community support officers mentions that the residential manager at the housing project complained about cars showing up in the area that she did not recognize (O). The cars and their drivers tended to hang around the abandoned community center in the heart of the housing project and near some homes that had been victimized (A and L). The community officer said that the residence manager had actually seen a couple of kids trying to break into a house through a set of patio doors. She scared them off and called the police, but they had gone by the time the patrol team arrived. She had seen them around and knew they were local kids (O).

The community support officer also mentions that on his recent visit to the high school the head teacher had noticed an increase in concerned parents (V). Amy phones the head teacher to offer some reassurance and seek more information, and the principal mentions that there has been an increase in the incidence of cars speeding past the school. The head teacher mentions that they have had an uptick in truancy with their more problematic students.

Some snippets of information may assist with more than one element of VOLTAGE, and there may also be VOLTAGE elements that are not particularly well fleshed out by the information that is available to Amy. But it is a good start, and Amy can now start to form some possible ideas (hypotheses) about what might be going on. She can even rule out some of the possible causes that emerged from her management meeting.

To help with this, Amy draws on a technique she learned during her military service. Intelligence analysts use a technique called Analysis of Competing Hypotheses that she decides to use (ACH, Box 4.7). A read of the information available to Amy starts to give her a clue about the likely veracity of some of the hunches (hypotheses) suggested to her in the management meeting and by others.

BOX 4.7 ANALYSIS OF COMPETING HYPOTHESES

Intelligence analysts sometimes formalize their thinking by conducting an analysis of competing hypotheses (ACH). It involves creating a matrix like the one shown here with the various pieces of evidence (in rows) available down the left side of the matrix. In each of the columns you note the different hypotheses (in four columns) that have been volunteered.

Going row by row, you next determine if the evidence confirms the hypothesis (✓), is inconsistent with the hypothesis (✗), or is neutral regarding the hypothesis (−).

		Hypotheses		
	MS-13 infiltration	Nighttime burglaries	Weekend louts	Local truants
Middle of the day during the week	−	✗	✗	✓
Heroin attracting outside users	−	−	✓	−
Local gang accepting property	✗	✓	✗	✓
Local gang sending local users to burgle	✗	✓	✗	✓
Unknown cars by community center	✓	−	✓	−
Local kids seen breaking into house	✗	✓	✗	✓

(Evidence is the label for the rows.)

Some pieces of evidence might be discarded at this point if they neither confirm nor disconfirm any hypotheses. The hypothesis that you should focus on is the one with the least number of inconsistencies, not the one with the most ticks. The table shows that *local truants* is the hypothesis most consistent with the available evidence.

Once you have a contender, take a moment to consider how sensitive the analysis is to specific pieces of evidence. This is important in case information has come from a questionable source (such as a potential Walt Disney). If your analysis still holds, you can consider the hypothesis with the least number of inconsistencies for further analysis. If you have multiple hypotheses that are plausible with few inconsistencies, you can try and identify possible intelligence gaps that, when filled, would distinguish between the hypotheses and reduce the ambiguity.

After reading Box 4.7, you might have concluded, like Amy, that local truants are the most likely cause of the problem. The next stage is to figure out what to do about the crime problem. Before rushing into an operational response, it will be useful to read the next two chapters that will:

1 help you understand why crime occurs
2 provide a primer on what police can do about it.

CHAPTER SUMMARY

- Get into the habit of engaging in a regular process of analysis for your crime and disorder problems.
- Unstructured thinking is inefficient and error prone.
- Use VOLTAGE to structure analysis (Victims, Offenders, Locations, Times, Attractors, Groups, Enhancers).
- Draw information from the three Cs: Crime analysis, Criminal intelligence, and Community information.
- Frame questions that are less descriptive but instead geared to learn why.
- Identify and use 'natural police' to gain insights, but be aware of 'Walt Disneys.'
- Remember the importance of conveying your interests and intent to analysts in the 4-i model.
- Compile your evidence and possible causes (hypotheses).
- Consider a structured technique like ACH and prioritize the hypothesis with the least number of inconsistencies.

NOTE

* In the original version of VOLTAGE from the second edition of my book on *Intelligence-Led Policing*, T referred to TREND because understanding the temporal trend of the crime problem is important. However, people generally refer to this component as TIMES and they find it easier to remember that way, so I've changed it to TIMES in this version of VOLTAGE.

REFERENCES

1 Jones, M.D., *The Thinker's Toolkit: 14 Powerful Techniques for Problem Solving.* 1998, New York: Random House.
2 Ratcliffe, J.H., *Intelligence-Led Policing (2nd edition).* 2016, Abingdon, Oxon.: Routledge. p. 310.
3 Chainey, S. and J.H. Ratcliffe, *GIS and Crime Mapping.* 2005, London: John Wiley and Sons.
4 IACP, *Confidential Informants and Information.* 2008, International Association of Chiefs of Police National Law Enforcement Policy Center: Elexandria, VA.
5 Derry, P., *Inside a Police Informant's Mind.* 2015, Boco Raton, FL: CRC Press.
6 Maguire, M. and T. John, *Intelligence, Surveillance and Informants: Integrated Approaches.* Police Research Group: Crime Detection and Prevention Series, 1995. Paper 64: p. 58.
7 Wensley, F.P., *Forty Years of Scotland Yard.* 1931, New York: Doubleday, Doran and Company.
8 Innes, M., et al., *Seeing like a citizen: field experiments in 'community intelligence-led policing.'* Police Practice and Research, 2009. **10**(2): p. 99–114.
9 President's Task Force on 21st Century Policing, *Final Report of the President's Task Force on 21st Century Policing.* 2015, Office of Community Oriented Policing Services; Washington, D.C.

5

UNDERSTANDING CRIME PATTERNS

WHAT CAUSES CRIME?

Most criminologists are more interested in criminals than in crime. They study and discuss theories about why someone becomes a criminal, how long they commit crime, and why some commit more than others. While this may be fascinating, most police officers are interested in preventing crime. If someone just punched you and ran off with your iPhone, it doesn't help knowing that he was often truant from school or that his father grew up in financial distress.

Fortunately for policing, in the early 1980s environmental criminologists and crime scientists became interested in crime opportunities at the point where crime occurred. The traditional (dispositional) view was that an offender's personal temperament to commit crime was the driving force in crime and disorder. Any attempts to prevent offending would simply displace crime. The ideas around opportunity were a rejection of this mainstream thinking, because they largely took the dispositional causes for granted, recognizing them as background or risk factors in explaining crime. Today's crime researchers are more interested in explaining why an offence happened at a particular place and time.

Opportunity plays a central role in explaining the patterns of crime we see in our society.

Opportunity plays a central role in explaining the patterns of crime we see in our society. The variation of opportunities, to some degree, explains why we have different levels of crime in places. Our travel patterns and habits, the weaknesses and opportunities in the physical or social fabric of our neighborhoods, and the attractiveness of certain targets all play a role. An appreciation for these factors can help you create crime reduction strategies. This chapter is an overview of these ideas.

Most police officers roll their eyes at a discussion of criminological theories, but please keep reading! While the majority of this chapter will be spent walking you through the important ones, the next section is a quick overview of more developmental issues in society and families. As a member of a crime reduction partnership, you will encounter many people who may want to discuss these types of causes, so a little background might be useful.

WHY DO INDIVIDUALS BECOME CRIMINALS?

While there is a resurgence of interest in biological criminology, we have moved on from the discredited ideas of the 19th century. You can't tell if someone is a criminal by measuring the size of their head. No respected researchers argue for genetic determinism; instead, they recognize that most human behavior is a complicated mix of biological, developmental, and situational factors. We can have a genetic disposition to certain behaviors, but these can be exacerbated or controlled by our upbringing or the particular situation in which we find ourselves. This nuanced mix of influences was appreciated by Frederick Wensley nearly 100 years ago (see Box 5.1).

BOX 5.1 CHIEF CONSTABLE WENSLEY ON ENVIRONMENT AND CIRCUMSTANCES

Chief Constable Wensley of the Criminal Investigation Department of Scotland Yard had a perspective on the structural factors that increased the likelihood an offender would end up in a life of crime, writing at the end of his career in 1931:

"Those forty-two years in the thick of the fight against crime have, I think, at least taught me to keep a balanced perspective. I have learned that the world is not so bad after all, and that even criminals have their good and bad points, very much like other people. It is not always their fault that conditions have molded them wrongly. With very few exceptions criminals are made by environment and circumstances. . . . They have, in some cases, been taught since childhood to regard robbery in one form or another as a natural thing; or their first plunge may have been taken through desperation, or through a boyish dislike of monotonous work and a wish to take a short cut to what they regard as the good things of life."[1]

The biosocial influence

Biosocial criminology now recognizes that there are genetic factors that can influence criminal behavior. These could be hormonal changes, neurological events (such as birth complications or traumatic brain injury), or even evolutionary causes. Evolutionary psychologists argue that hundreds of thousands of years of evolutionary selection can partially explain why men are more prone to violence, and adolescents are more likely to engage in risky behavior. Biosocial criminologists have used genetic studies of twins to suggest that "antisocial behavior is around 50 percent heritable."[2]

But crime is about much more than genetics. The environment certainly seems to moderate anti-social behavior. Strain theory argues that some people are drawn to crime because they do not have access to economic goals and suffer relative deprivation. In other words, they can feel entitled to more than they have and take action to remedy the situation, turning to crime. This can cause not only property crime, but also violence and disorder as they strike out against the injustices of their school, family life, peers, or social status.[3] Negative behavior can be exacerbated by a weak commitment to societal values, or they may have criminal friends or gang membership, and have the opportunity and skills to commit crime.

Some of these strains can be aspects that we can all appreciate (such as being poorer than other people) while others are more subjective to the individual (such as having fewer opportunities for advancement than other people at the same social level). Some wealthier people experience strain because they set goals for themselves that are too lofty.[3] Individuals can set lower expectations for themselves and reduce their stress. This might explain the lower crime rate among first generation immigrants to many Western countries: they set or have greater tolerance for low economic goals.

The developmental influence

As we enter adolescence and puberty, we undergo significant biological and cognitive changes. This displays itself in the age-crime curve that—while not explaining every offender's behavior—is a reliable aggregate behavior predictor. Basically, anti-social behavior starts in adolescence, peaks around 17 years of age, and declines into adulthood. This pattern is evident across most cultures and nations, demonstrated here with Canadian data (see Figure 5.1). Adolescence is a time when we seek out risky and rewarding experiences—especially when with friends and peers.[4]

> Anti-social behavior starts in adolescence, peaks around 17 years of age, and declines into adulthood.

Rate per 100,000 population of individuals accused of crime

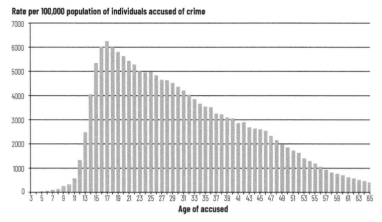

Figure 5.1 The classic age-crime curve of offending and age

Source: Statistics Canada

The developmental and life-course (DLC) perspective in criminology comprises a whole swathe of theories around offending lifestyles and criminal behavior. It concerns itself with why people start, continue, and then eventually stop offending. In other words, the *onset, persistence,* and *desistence* of offending behavior.[5]

Some of the key findings have concerned the influence of family disruption caused by parents and grandparents displaying antisocial behavior, or being exposed to violence. These can influence a developing child's abilities to interact with others and learn from social interaction in either positive or anti-social ways. Poor socioeconomic status and aggressive tendencies can tilt the balance towards anti-social behavior. Offenders can emerge from their criminal career if certain 'turning points' can provide a positive influence (such as marriage, joining the military, or moving neighborhood). Equally, divorce, domestic violence, or loss of employment can increase criminal behavior. If offenders see the world as unfair or corrupt or alienating towards them, they can persist in their criminal careers.[6]

The situational influence

The situations that the offender is faced with, and how they behave in certain circumstances, are considered by the opportunity theories, and situational action theory.[7] The opportunity theories are so important for policing that most of the rest of this chapter is dedicated to them. But for now, we will briefly discuss situational action theory.

The idea works like this. People can be motivated to undertake an action (such as a crime) mainly because they are tempted or provoked into action. This propensity for crime is influenced by their personal moral code as well as ability (or not) to exercise self-control. So, according to situational action theory, a person's motivation to commit a crime is driven by *temptation* and/or *provocation* but tempered by the person's *moral filter*. This moral filter is influenced by the perceived moral standards of the setting. In other words, if everyone at the party is smoking pot, then this suggests that the moral norms of the party don't exactly frown on recreational drug use.

If someone sees crime as a viable option, they may act out of habit (a *habitual decision* might be someone who is violent when drunk) or more deliberately (a *deliberate decision* might be to shoplift when the store clerk's attention is elsewhere). When acting deliberately, it may be possible to influence their behavior. They can be encouraged to exercise self-control or influenced by the presence of some form of deterrence.

The policing challenge with individual influences

While all of these theories are interesting to a degree, it is difficult to know how to respond to them from the view of the police service. In other words, *so what?* Because we don't live in a totalitarian dictatorship (apologies to readers from North Korea), there is little societal enthusiasm for police to engage in social engineering. We don't incarcerate people because they have certain genetic propensities, and we don't conduct surveillance on people because they witnessed domestic abuse as a child.

One area where local area commanders may be able to exert influence is in the situational arena. We can't determine people's moral filter, but we may be able to control the provocations and temptations they encounter. And we can also influence the distribution of deterrence resources. Understanding the various scales of situational crime is therefore important for understanding how offenders take advantage of opportunities, as the next section explains.

OPPORTUNITY CAUSES CRIME

We are all creatures of habit. As Hannibal Lecter says in *The Silence of the Lambs*: "We begin by coveting what we see every day." Most people take the same route to and from work, at a similar time every day. We head to a selection of the same bars and restaurants, shop at the usual supermarket on the weekend, and go to our favorite movie theater with friends. We follow these similar patterns of behavior for convenience, efficiency, and routine. We also do these at roughly the same time of day because we are constrained by factors such as office hours, school times, and the dash to happy hour. These are the routine activities of our lives.

Routine activities theory

The routine activities theory (also known as the routine activity approach) has, since Marcus Felson and his co-author introduced it in 1979,[8] remained a cornerstone to understanding crime. For a crime to occur, there has to be a convergence of:

- a likely offender
- a suitable target and
- the absence of a capable guardian.

The likely offender is anyone who is inclined to commit crime. The suitable target could refer to any object or person that could be attacked or taken by the offender. The capable guardian does not necessarily refer to the police, but also perhaps a teacher, parent, or nightclub bouncer. The capable guardian is anyone whose presence would inhibit offending behavior. The combination of these three components (likely offender, suitable target, and absence of capable guardian) provides the chemistry necessary for a crime to occur. Felson has continued to develop and expand his theory,[9] but this simple explanation remains its foundation.

If you think about it for a moment, human behavior can explain many of the spatial and temporal patterns of crime. For example, since World War II it has become more commonplace in developed countries for all adults in a household to work. With the kids at school, this has resulted in more empty households during the day. When do most residential burglaries occur? During the daytime in the work week. When and where do acts of alcohol-fueled violence tend to concentrate? Friday and Saturday nights in bar and entertainment districts when more people are out drinking at the end of the working week.

These are examples of aggregate criminal behavior. In other words, in general criminal behavior tends to occur at broadly predictable times and places and in non-random ways. There are always exceptions because we are dealing with human behavior. I once had a challenging time trying to arrest a very large and violent drunk at 9.30am on a Friday morning behind Mile End tube station in London; however, my experience was most unusual for that time of day. It is more common for offenders (and victims) to follow predictable patterns. This aggregate criminal behavior can be useful to police operations (see, for example, Box 5.2). Because of its ability to explain larger scale criminal patterns—and our likelihood of victimization—the routine activities approach is generally considered a macro-level explanation for crime.

BOX 5.2 USING CRIME THEORY TO CRACK A ROBBERY RING

"I supervised a plainclothes unit whose job included catching suspects in the act of committing burglaries, thefts, and robberies. We used our understanding of routine activities theory to focus on an area and time where robberies had recently occurred, a neighborhood with dozens of bars next to a large residential area. We positioned ourselves based on what we knew about the potential victims, their paths home, and likely access route for suspects. With only six officers, we focused our efforts in a three-block area and watched for someone fleeing to the freeway a short distance away. We watched the poorly-lit residential streets next to the bars and the intoxicated people walking home.

This strategy paid off. One night, two of my officers observed offenders fleeing from their second robbery of the night to a nearby getaway car. The rest of us immediately positioned ourselves on the most likely egress routes out of the neighborhood. The suspects were stopped and arrested after a brief pursuit. Robberies in the area declined significantly immediately afterwards."

Sergeant Steve Bishopp is a patrol supervisor with the Dallas Police Department, Texas (U.S.). He has a Ph.D. from the University of Texas at Dallas.

Crime pattern theory

Crime pattern theory transfers the larger, macro-level ideas of the routine activities approach to a more neighborhood level explanation for crime. While the movies like to portray 'hunting' criminals, the reality is usually more mundane. Like non-criminals, offenders move regularly around their neighborhood between home, school, shopping, bars, and so forth, often for non-criminal journeys. This area becomes the location where they also seek criminal opportunities, and as a result, crime clusters in this area.[10] It's called the offender's awareness space. When the awareness spaces of offenders overlap with easy criminal opportunities, we often see higher levels of crime.

Crime is rarely random but rather a combination of the awareness spaces of offenders and the opportunities for crime they encounter.

The supply of likely offenders and criminal opportunities is not static and can change by place and time.[11] Offenders may be more attracted to shoplift from a dollar store because they shop there regularly and it's in their awareness space. They never visit the high-end deli and are thus unaware that it might be a prime target. The environmental backcloth can also change in myriad and dynamic ways. A corner-store that usually has two nighttime employees might have one out sick and is now more vulnerable to robbery, or a bar that attracts cash-in-hand workers may have more potential for fights and drunken mayhem on payday. Crime is rarely random but rather a combination of the awareness spaces of offenders and the opportunities for crime they encounter.

Rational choice perspective

A complementary idea to routine activities and crime pattern theory is the rational choice perspective. Like routine activities, this idea was a rejection of most mainstream criminological theories of the time—ideas that assumed situational crime prevention would simply displace crime with no net benefit.[12]

The basic premise is that crime is a relatively purposive decision about the perceived reward versus the risk. In other words, the offender considers whether the benefits of the crime he is about to commit outweigh the chances of being caught. The reward is often financial, but could also be a benefit in terms of sex, excitement, or status with peers. The perceived reward might not make much sense to us, but it does to the offender. Also bear in mind that the risk is the likelihood of getting caught, *as perceived by the criminal*, not the actual risk.

These decisions may not be entirely rational. They are often constrained by time (the rush to make a decision when faced with an opportunity) or what limited information is available about the risk. This bounded rationality can also be affected by exposure to drugs or alcohol. In some circumstances, offenders can display a breathtaking lack of rationality. These shining examples of the Dunning-Kruger effect are often arrested quickly (see Box 5.3).

BOX 5.3 THE DUNNING-KRUGER EFFECT: "BUT I WORE THE JUICE"

The Dunning-Kruger effect is named after the research of American social psychologists David Dunning and Justin Kruger. It happens when people are basically too incompetent to know they aren't good at something. Dunning and Kruger recount the hilarious tale of 44-year-old McArthur Wheeler, who in 1995 decided to rob a couple of banks in Pittsburgh, Pennsylvania. Because Wheeler had learned that lemon juice can be used for invisible writing (it becomes visible when the paper is held near a source of heat), he reckoned that by smearing his face with lemon juice he would be invisible to security cameras. So that's what he did. Apparently, he even confirmed the success of his invisibility by taking a selfie with a Polaroid camera. He was arrested shortly after police showed bank surveillance video on the evening news. During interview, Wheeler was genuinely stunned that his trick had failed. "But I wore the juice," he mumbled.[13]

Not only does this story demonstrate that Wheeler wasn't even smart enough to take a selfie, it is also a good example of the illusory superiority bias (the Dunning-Kruger effect). This occurs when people hold overly optimistic and deluded impressions of their own abilities. Particularly incompetent people not only make inaccurate conclusions about their skills; worse, their incompetence leaves them unable to realize it. Or, to put it another way, some people are just too stupid to know how stupid they are.

The rational choice perspective encourages us to think about a crime-specific approach because it explicitly examines the situational components of the crime. This makes sense to many police officers because we have all experienced opportunist offenders. These are the guys that will steal from an unlocked car, assault and rob a drunk unable to defend themselves, or commit credit card fraud if they can get away with it. While their broader motivations to get involved in crime might come from a group of causes we can't influence, the situation of each specific crime will dictate what they do.

Speaking of broader motivations, rational choice recognizes this distinction between the *criminal involvement* decision (to become a criminal) and the *criminal event* decision (to steal from an unlocked car). We can't usually influence the former, but we can do something about the latter. By understanding opportunities, we can work to prevent them. Because of this focus on the immediate criminal event, rational choice is a micro-level explanation for crime.

The scale of opportunities

Reading the previous section, you might have noticed that the three theories dovetail with each other nicely. Broad routine activity patterns create the chemistry necessary for crime to occur. At the neighborhood level, the crime patterns are where offenders come into contact with these opportunities in their day-to-day lives, and specifically the awareness spaces that are formed through their routine activities. And when faced with an opportunity, at the micro-level scale of the criminal opportunity, an offender (who has previously made a criminal involvement decision to be open to committing crime) has to make a criminal event decision. Will he smash a vehicle window to steal the computer from the front seat of the car, or punch the guy that just jostled him at the bar and made him spill his pint? This rational choice (or more likely *bounded rationality* at the bar) takes place at the very place and time where the crime is likely to occur.

With this understanding in place, you can see that the VOLTAGE components (Chapter 4) are designed to help you appreciate different possible opportunities that might generate a crime hot spot. If the bar serves too many drunk patrons, then the jostler and the offender may both be too inebriated to avoid each other (L, V, and E). If local residents are too relaxed about leaving valuables in their cars, then theft opportunities are created (V and L). And if the bar serves alcohol later than others, then a last-minute rush for drinks on a weekend can cause more pressure (L and T).

In these examples, concrete crime reduction strategies exist. Residents can be reminded to secure their valuables, and the bar can be asked (or mandated) to close at the same time as others, not serve visibly drunk patrons, and move tables away from the bar to reduce congestion. The three main opportunity theories can be converted to practical crime reduction as we will see in the next chapter.

NEIGHBORHOODS AND CRIME ATTRACTORS

Whenever in a new place doing training or consulting with a police department, I always ask for a few bar recommendations from the troops. Police officers are the best people to ask. In most towns, I can get a good heads-up on a brew pub or a nice place to take my partner, if she is with me. It's also useful to learn where to avoid. Ask a room full of cops which is the worst bar in town and you usually get a heated discussion about the best place to get robbed, become embroiled in an old-school bar fight, or witness a stabbing.

These harmful components of neighborhoods are important for police to try and address. Witnessing poor *social-interaction mechanisms* (like kids being forced to conform to adverse social norms around these unhealthy places) can be as harmful as *environmental mechanisms* like exposure to violence, graffiti, and decay. Social stigmatization of a neighborhood occurs and businesses flee.[14] The few businesses that remain can become crime generators or attractors.

Places that are poorly designed or don't control the number of people crammed into the bar for happy hour (for example) often become crime generators—places that *inadvertently* create crime opportunities.[15] Large numbers of people come without the specific intent of committing crime, but then take advantage of opportunities that are too good to miss. Examples include shopping malls, sports stadiums, and train and bus stations.

Crime attractors can appear similar to crime generators, but are places that offenders are *deliberately* drawn to because of the criminal opportunities. Areas where drugs are sold or prostitutes work are examples of crime attractors. Some stores are designed so poorly that offenders target them specifically for shoplifting. By skimping on protection or the number of shop assistants, the shops can become risky facilities.[17]

We see similar characteristics in other areas of police business. For years, the Bloor Street Viaduct in Toronto was one of the most popular bridges in the world from which to commit suicide, second only to the Golden Gate Bridge in San Francisco. When the authorities installed a suicide barrier in 2003, they removed the easy opportunity. Suicides from the bridge dropped by 90 percent, and didn't displace to nearby bridges.[16]

Much of your work as an area commander will involve working in neighborhoods and communities. Use the A in VOLTAGE to consider what crime and disorder problems you have that might be caused by opportunities deriving from crime generators or attractors (and note that the A in VOLTAGE is used to cover both crime attractors and crime generators). They are important because there is often a direct link between these places and chronic problems.

Protective factors and controlling influences

While you are considering the VOLTAGE A, also be aware that your neighborhood may have some protective factors that can be encouraged. While we have likely offenders and suitable targets, we can counteract them by encouraging handlers, guardians, and place managers.[9]

Handlers are people who can exert a controlling effect on potential offenders. For example, while kids can get in trouble walking home from school, they are less likely to do so if the school requires a parent to accompany them. Teachers can patrol a playground and provide a controlling influence. And you have probably experienced, like me, the pressure to drive more courteously when your mother is in the car! If the handlers are not present, or are too weak to exert any real influence, then problems can be encouraged.

Guardians can protect victims from crime. There are formal guardians, such as police officers and security guards, but be open to exploiting informal guardianship as well. Encouraging friends to escort drunk compatriots home from the bar, or asking neighbors to collect mail when folk are away are ways to extend the notion of guardianship.

Place managers are the third category. These are people who live or work at a place and can extend some protection to surrounding areas where crime might occur. Most places are owned by somebody, and these owners—and the people who work for them—are potential place managers, even if crime prevention is not their primary responsibility. Beach lifeguards are present to prevent drowning, but they can also keep

Figure 5.2 The crime triangle

an eye out for crime. In the same way, motel clerks or park employees can exercise some place management around where they work.

The relationship between all of these factors is shown in Figure 5.2. The crime triangle shows that a crime problem occurs when an offender interacts with a target or victim at a place. We can control the elements of crime by upsetting this dynamic. For example, we can introduce a guardian to protect the victim, use a manager to control a place, or find a handler who can influence the behavior of an offender. Always keep the crime triangle in mind when thinking about VOLTAGE.

A focus on place is a good starting point

I'm aware that you probably have a larger crime problem than exists on a single street block, but researchers are starting to understand more about the importance of street blocks (we are talking here about both sides of a street between two intersections). It's where behavior is formed and regulated—what academics call a *behavior setting*. Residents of a block get to know one another and their routines, and certain people take on roles such as block captain or busybody. The block forms the rules and determines what constitutes acceptable behavior on that block. While all of this can be dynamic and changing, many of these block norms are quite enduring.[18,19] Street blocks can have stable crime profiles that can last for years.[20] Many people in policing have this implicit understanding, which is why it's nice to see research confirming it. And why we often see police leaders try to reclaim a city 'one block at a time.'

Chances are, there is no singular context that dominates the causal mechanisms of crime. There may even be forces at the neighborhood level that drive crime at the street level, and problems on blocks that infect a wider community.[21] With some crime problems, the challenges are at a place like a nuisance bar or with a troubled family. Others might involve a group of blocks that has an ongoing problem containing violence, or a housing complex that is overrun by a gang problem. Good crime prevention starts by understanding the scale of your problem and trying to narrow down the real trouble to the smallest place possible. When your colleagues tell you than an entire neighborhood is a crime-ridden wasteland, be suspicious. The evidence overwhelmingly suggests there are good and bad pockets in even the worst places.

DISPLACEMENT AND WHY DRUG MARKETS ARE LIKE FAST FOOD RESTAURANTS

When I'm conducting training with police officers, someone always brings up the issue of displacement. It is an assumed truism in policing that if we stop crime in one place, it will just move around the corner. Fortunately, there is so little evidence of full crime displacement from successful crime reduction that I once wrote a paper called 'Burglary reduction and the myth of displacement.'[22]

The following analogy might help. A street-corner drug market has many of the hallmarks of a fast-food restaurant. They are both looking to move into neighborhoods that do not have the social cohesion to resist them, and have lots of potential customers. It is also beneficial if they are close to main roads so they can get some regional traffic. If we can deny either type of business their prime location then, yes, they will probably move somewhere else. After all, people seem to want drugs as much as burgers and milkshakes. But the next place the businesses move to will not be as good as the first, otherwise they would have been there to begin with. So their second location is a bit less successful, and they will sell fewer drugs (or burgers). If we can deny them this second location, they will move another time, but again will end up in an even less desirable spot. Each time they move, we see a reduction in community harm.

The research evidence supports this. Across more than 100 studies, there is scant evidence of complete spatial displacement.[23] Where a crime reduction initiative has had some success, we rarely see a situation where all of that crime has moved to nearby areas. And while some displacement is seen in about one quarter of cases, we see just as often the reverse—a diffusion of benefits. This happens when the benefits of a crime operation spillover to nearby locations that were not part of the initiative. This 'halo effect' occurs for a variety of reasons, but has been found to be more prevalent than crime displacement (see Box 5.4).[24]

BOX 5.4 EXAMPLES OF A DIFFUSION OF BENEFITS

In Jersey City (U.S.) police targeted a drug-infested area known as Storms Avenue and a prostitution location on Cornelison Avenue. Police patrols, narcotics enforcement, and situational crime prevention were employed in the specific areas. Not only did crime decline in the target areas, but also in the surrounding roads. The prostitutes and drug dealers complained that they couldn't move to a new location nearby because the "money won't be the same" and "it takes time to build up customers." Others explained that they didn't move and preferred to stay near home because it was their 'turf.' They were, in effect, constrained by their routine activities and their awareness spaces.[25]

Diffusion of benefits has even been found in non-spatial settings. When Caller-ID was introduced in the U.S. state of New Jersey, it allowed someone answering a phone to see the number of the caller. It was designed as a way of reducing obscene and nuisance calls. We take this convenience for granted now, but when it was introduced only about 2 percent of telephone subscribers had the technology. Criminologist Ron Clarke found that annoying phone calls declined by up to 20 percent, most likely because callers had no idea whether the number they were calling had the technology.[26]

SOCIAL NETWORKS ARE IMPORTANT

While this chapter has so far shown that crime is not random, neither are a criminal's social networks. Individuals, unless complete lone wolves, are part of larger social groups that can influence their offending behavior. A significant shoplifting ring operated in Camden, New Jersey (U.S.) for years before being broken up by detectives. It was comprised of hundreds of people stealing to order for a network of corner stores. They were all recruited via social connections among mostly drug users (see Box 5.5).

BOX 5.5 OPERATION BULLSEYE

Operation Bullseye dismantled a large shoplifting operation responsible for shoplifting millions of dollars of merchandize. Law enforcement detectives worked with private sector investigators (mainly from the Target company) over six months to take down a network of thieves organized by some corner stores (known locally as bodegas) in the City of Camden, New Jersey (U.S.). The bodega operators maintained a network of hundreds of thieves who would target big box stores, shoplifting specific desirable and requested items. The bodegas would accept the stolen merchandize and ship it to other cities, such as New York City.

The *boosters* (termed because, unlike shoplifters, they don't keep the stolen goods for themselves) were recruited by connections through social networks, often of drug users. Because boosters were recruited by word-of-mouth from connections, the network was challenging for law enforcement to penetrate. It is likely that many of the offenders would not have been such prolific boosters if they had not had a convenient system of bodegas ready to trade stolen goods for cash. Operation Bullseye demonstrates the power of social networks to create criminal opportunities for offenders.

Sources: Target and Camden County investigators (personal conversations) and www.nj.com/ south/index.ssf/2008/11/task_force_breaks_shoplifting.html

---

Networks have been shown to be influential in the development of, at one end, victimization patterns, and, at the other end, terrorist cells, gangs, computer hacker communities, and drug traffickers.[27] Research on gangs and drug networks has demonstrated the importance of people with *social capital* (structural position) versus *human capital* (access to resources). It is useful to know the social status of individuals within their gang or group if you want to tailor effective focused deterrence strategies (see next chapter). In particular, law enforcement can:

1   Identify the social network of rivalries and alliances among street gangs so that you can select certain groups for enforcement or other intervention. Tackling gangs that are embedded

in feuds with other groups might stem violence by removing one of the key driving forces.

2 Determine the street gang network's cohesion in order to estimate the impact of a strategy. For example, if a focused deterrence approach (see next chapter) is to be adopted, it will be more effective with gangs that have high levels of cohesion. With low cohesion groups the strategy might actually backfire.

3 Identify the *brokers* within the street gangs. These key players occupy positions of leverage (sometimes known as 'cut points') that can be vulnerable to intervention programs. Removing or influencing these people can send a significant message to the wider criminal group.

4 Accept the likelihood that some street gang networks include participants who are not traditional gang members. As such, these people may still be intervention opportunities even if they are in the legitimate workforce.[28]

5 Conduct a gang (or drug dealing network) audit to identify which groups are more susceptible to perpetrating or being victims of violence.[29]

This is where street sources and criminal intelligence resources can help with the G part of your VOLTAGE analysis. Seek out connections (in your social network) who can help you understand the dynamics of the networks you are trying to dismantle or disrupt. A gang audit can be an excellent way to gather criminal intelligence from various sources. Furthermore, the victimization prevention message can resonate with community partners.

MOST CRIME IS LOCAL

Most police chiefs think that their area is a net importer of offenders. There is a simple explanation for this. When they look at the home address of the people they arrest, they see some people from outside their jurisdiction, and so think their town is a criminal attractor. What they do not see are the offenders who live in their town and are arrested somewhere else.

City-to-city offenders tend to be rarer than people think. When working in Canberra, Australia, a police superintendent once tried to convince me that their big problem was criminals from Sydney traveling down to Canberra (a three-hour drive) to break into houses and steal televisions. I was surprised he didn't question why there could be such a shortage of televisions in Australia's largest city. Of course, the superintendent's belief had been influenced by a couple of offenders who gave their home address in Sydney.

The (aggregate criminal behavior) research is clear. Offenders do not travel far to commit crime. Long distances are too much effort. Instead, crooks tend to focus on their own neighborhood and even their own streets (their awareness space). The influence of these routine activity patterns can also be seen in victimization: half the people shot in Philadelphia are shot within two blocks of their home address.[30] The same people are often victimized, as are schools and certain retail establishments. Repeat victimization studies indicate that once a home has been the victim of a burglary it has an increased chance of being targeted again for a number of weeks. Worse, near repeat victimization is also a driver in local crime patterns. What does this mean? When a home is burgled, not only is the original house at greater risk for a number of weeks (repeat victimization) but surrounding homes are also at increased risk for a few weeks. It's a form of crime contagion. It may be caused by offenders gaining more experience in a particular area, and also sharing their knowledge with co-offenders. The near repeat phenomenon has been found with burglaries, vehicle crime, and even in patterns of improvised explosive device attacks on coalition forces in Iraq.

There are some types of crime where distance is not as predictable, such as internet crimes like cyber-stalking and online grooming. However, in general, offenders are most likely to be local. A smart and well-trained crime analyst can be a real asset in understanding these local crime patterns (see Box 5.6).

BOX 5.6 THE ROLE OF ANALYSTS IN MODERN POLICING

"After running our crime analysis unit, I returned to patrol. Issues included a spike in stolen vehicles, a neighborhood on the outskirts of our precinct which had serious livability issues and felt they were being underserved by us, and lastly a shopping center in which several chain businesses were talking about leaving due to shoplifting.

Luckily, I still had great contacts with our crime analysis unit. They were able to identify our most prolific car thieves for our street crimes unit to target. For the neighborhood issues, we worked with the analysts to run a neighborhood survey, identified the primary concerns, and had our neighborhood response team respond. The survey alone helped the residents feel their needs were being addressed. Tackling the issues was then the icing on the cake. Finally, the analysts mapped the locations and identified the days and times the crimes were occurring at the shopping center. The holidays were coming up so we organized a series of walking patrols where officers focused on the times and locations with the most problems, but also interacted with shoppers, building community relations.

We used analysis to identify prolific offenders, conduct surveys, map crime locations and times, and even identify some crime series occurring at the mall. It helped us match our responses specifically to the issues. We were even able to leverage the crime reduction efforts to improve our relationship with our residents."

Greg Stewart is currently a sergeant with the Portland (Oregon) Police Bureau's North Precinct (U.S.).

CHAPTER SUMMARY

- Biosocial and developmental factors can partly influence a person's criminal involvement decision, but there are limited policing applications to these factors.
- Situational factors and the availability of opportunities drive the criminal event decision.
- The routine activities theory requires a likely offender, a suitable target, and the absence of a capable guardian for a crime to occur.
- The rational choice perspective states that the offender considers whether the benefits of the crime he is about to commit outweigh the risk of being caught.
- Sometimes this rationality will be bounded by exposure to drugs, alcohol, or the constraints of time, limiting the offender's decision-making capacity.
- Crime attractors and crime generators can concentrate crime problems in your area.
- The crime triangle explains the chemistry of crime, and what might be done about it.
- Crime displacement is a potential benefit and can deflect offending to less harmful areas. A diffusion of benefits is equally possible.
- It is useful to know the networks and social status of individuals within their gang or group to enable tailoring of effective focused strategies.
- Most crime is local and offenders do not travel far to commit crime.

REFERENCES

1   Wensley, F.P., *Forty Years of Scotland Yard*. 1931, New York: Doubleday, Doran and Company.

2   Barnes, J.C., B.B. Boutwell, and K.M. Beaver, *Contemporary biosocial criminology*, in *The Handbook of Criminological Theory*, A.R. Piquero, Editor. 2015, John Wiley and Sons: West Sussex. p. 75–99.

3   Agnew, R., *Strain, economic status, and crime*, in *The Handbook of Criminological Theory*, A.R. Piquero, Editor. 2015, John Wiley and Sons: West Sussex. p. 209–229.

4 Cauffman, E., et al., *A developmental perspective on adolescent risk-taking and criminal behavior*, in *The Handbook of Criminological Theory*, A.R. Piquero, Editor. 2015, John Wiley and Sons: West Sussex. p. 100–20.

5 Piquero, A.R., T.R. McGee, and D.P. Farrington, *Developmental and life-course theories of crime*, in *The Handbook of Criminological Theory*, A.R. Piquero, Editor. 2015, John Wiley and Sons: West Sussex. p. 336–54.

6 Laub, J.H. and R.J. Sampson, *Shared Beginnings, Divergent Lives*. 2006, Cambridge, MA: Harvard University Press.

7 Wikström, P.-O.H. and K. Treiber, *Situational theory*, in *The Handbook of Criminological Theory*, A.R. Piquero, Editor. 2015, John Wiley and Sons: West Sussex. p. 415–44.

8 Cohen, L.E. and M. Felson, *Social change and crime rate trends: A routine activity approach*. American Sociological Review, 1979. **44**: p. 588–608.

9 Felson, M. and M.A. Eckert, *Crime and Everyday Life*, (5th edition). 2015, Thousand Oaks, California: Pine Forge Press.

10 Brantingham, P.L. and P.J. Brantingham, *Mobility, notoriety, and crime: A study in the crime patterns of urban nodal points*. Journal of Environmental Systems, 1981–2. **11**(1): p. 89–99.

11 Brantingham, P.L. and P.J. Brantingham, *Environment, routine, and situation: Toward a pattern theory of crime*, in *Routine Activity and Rational Choice*, R.V. Clarke and M. Felson, Editors. 1993, Transaction publishers: New Brunswick, NJ. p. 259–94.

12 Clarke, R.V. and M. Felson, *Introduction: Criminology, routine activity, and rational choice*, in *Routine Activity and Rational Choice*, R.V. Clarke and M. Felson, Editors. 1993, Transaction publishers: New Brunswick, NJ. p. 1–14.

13 Kruger, J. and D. Dunning, *Unskilled and unaware of it: How difficulties in recognizing one's own incompetence lead to inflated self-assessments*. Journal of Personality and Social Psychology, 1999. **77**(6): p. 1121–34.

14 Galster, G.C., *The mechanism(s) of neighborhood effects: Theory, evidence, and policy implications*, in *Neighbourhood Effects Research: New Perspectives*, M. van Ham, et al., Editors. 2012, Springer: London. p. 23–56.

15 Brantingham, P.L. and P.J. Brantingham, *Criminality of place: Crime generators and crime attractors*. European Journal of Criminal Policy and Research, 1995. **3**(3): p. 5–26.

16 Sinyor, M., et al., *Did the suicide barrier work after all? Revisiting the Bloor Viaduct natural experiment and its impact on suicide rates in Toronto*. BMJ Open, 2017. **7**(5): p. e015299.

17 Clarke, R.V. and J. Eck, *Crime analysis for problem solvers: In 60 small steps*. 2005, Washington, D.C.: Center for Problem Oriented Policing.

18 Taylor, R.B., *Social order and disorder of street blocks and neighborhoods: Ecology, microecology, and the systematic model of social disorganization*. Journal of Research in Crime and Delinquency, 1997. **34**(1): p. 113–55.

19 Taylor, R.B., *Breaking Away From Broken Windows*. 2001, Boulder, CO: Westview.

20 Weisburd, D., E.R. Groff, and S.-M. Yang, *The Criminology of Place: Street Segments and Our Understanding of the Crime Problem*. 2012, Oxford: Oxford University Press.

21 Taylor, R.B., *Community Criminology: Fundamentals of Spatial and Temporal Scaling, Ecological Indicators and Selectivity Bias*. 2015, New York: New York University Press.

22 Ratcliffe, J.H., *Burglary reduction and the myth of displacement*. Trends and Issues in Crime and Criminal Justice, 2002. No. 232.

23 Guerette, R.T. and K.J. Bowers, *Assessing the extent of crime displacement and diffusion of benefits: A review of situational crime prevention evaluations*. Criminology, 2009. **47**(4): p. 1331–68.

24 Gash, T., *The Hidden Forces of Crime Control*, in *On Second Thought*. 2017, North Dakota Humanities Council. p. 26–33.

25 Weisburd, D., et al., *Does crime just move around the corner? A controlled study of spatial diffusion and diffusion of crime control benefits*. Criminology, 2006. **44**(3): p. 549–91.

26 Clarke, R.V. and D. Weisburd, *Diffusion of crime control benefits*, in *Crime Prevention Studies*, R.V. Clarke, Editor. 1994, Criminal Justice Press: Monsey, NY. p. 165–83.

27 Malm, A.E. and G. Bichler, *Why networks?*, in *Disrupting Criminal Networks: Network Analysis in Crime Prevention*, G. Bichler and A.E. Malm, Editors. 2015, Lynne Rienner: Boulder, CO. p. 1–8.

28 McGloin, J.M. and Z. Rowan, *Street gangs and co-offending networks*, in *Disrupting Criminal Networks: Network Analysis in Crime Prevention*, G. Bichler and A.E. Malm, Editors. 2015, Lynne Rienner: Boulder, CO. p. 9–25.

29 Sierra-Arevalo, M. and A.V. Papachristos, *Applying group audits to problem-oriented policing*, in *Disrupting Criminal Networks: Network Analysis in Crime Prevention*, G. Bichler and A.E. Malm, Editors. 2015, Lynne Rienner: Boulder, CO. p. 27–46.

30 Ratcliffe, J.H. and G.F. Rengert, *Near repeat patterns in Philadelphia shootings*. Security Journal, 2008. **21**(1–2): p. 58–76.

6

HOW THE POLICE CAN IMPACT CRIME

FOCUS ON WHAT CAN BE ACHIEVED

Let's start by getting a few things straight about crime reduction. As we saw in Chapter 5, there are a number of reasons why a person becomes a criminal, but the police can't do much about them. You also read that a lot of crime is local, made possible by easier opportunities and conditions than at other places. As Jack Maple, a famous NYPD chief detective wrote: "When cops run into a chronic condition, they have two courses of action from which to choose: They can pick off the predators attracted by the prevailing conditions or they can try to change the prevailing conditions."[1]

To demonstrate the power of prevailing conditions, consider this question. If we removed all situational constraints on crime, such as locks, bars on windows, and passenger screening at airports, would crime increase? If you just said 'yes,' then you recognize the benefits of crime prevention. If you think about it for a moment, your response assumes that crime doesn't simply displace (as many cops argue). It waxes and wanes with the availability of opportunities. The majority of this chapter will concentrate on what can be achieved to control opportunities and where we have some chances to influence. We start, however, by reviewing a few avenues that are less likely to help.

THINGS THAT YOU SHOULDN'T RELY ON

Don't rely on the criminal justice system

Because police academies over-emphasize teaching the law to new police officers, some go on to have too much faith in the criminal justice system to solve society's woes. The flow of the criminal justice system you see in Figure 6.1 is a generalization, but it demonstrates the limits of that system. Using survey and official figures, the funnel was based on a sample of 1,000 crimes experienced by the public.[2] While your jurisdiction is likely to have some differences in the ratios down the funnel, those differences are probably less than you might suspect. In general, crime reporting, detection, prosecution, conviction, and imprisonment rates are steady because they are determined by largely static factors, such as public reporting practices and availability of resources like jail space.

The crime funnel is so named because as cases fall through the system, the numbers shrink. For every 1,000 crimes the public suffer, we incarcerate offenders in just four cases. As a result, we need to intervene higher in the crime funnel.[2] Improvements across the entire criminal justice system are important, but focusing closer to the top of the funnel will generate better returns on our investment of time and resources.

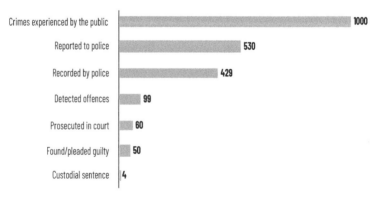

Figure 6.1 The crime funnel

Crime prevention acts at the top of the funnel, maximizing the impact of your work. This isn't to say that detections are not important. Far from it. They have value in a number of ways, and can bring an important sense of justice to crime victims. Policies that stress detections and prosecutions send a signal that may help people retain faith in the criminal justice system; however, numerous studies have repeatedly shown little evidence that general arrest and prosecution strategies significantly impact on crime.[3]

For every 1,000 crimes the public suffer, we incarcerate offenders in just four cases.

Think about detections as an opportunity to learn about offenders, and the opportunities they exploit. An offender interview is a marvelous chance to identify what weaknesses they took advantage of and what decisions they made. You can use it to fill intelligence gaps in your VOLTAGE analysis (see Chapter 4). Focusing on serious, repeat offenders is therefore valuable in a number of ways, but expecting the criminal justice system to solve our crime problems is not.

Don't rely on a strategy that isn't working

When Darth Vader told the commanding officer that the Emperor was coming to view progress of the Death Star's construction, Commander Jerjerrod replied "We shall double our efforts!" These days, the lack of resources available to area commanders rules out that option. And doubling the use of ineffective tactics is just making things worse. The situation can be exacerbated if you inherited a chronic problem from your predecessor, because you probably also inherited operational tactics that don't work. I'm often perplexed to see officers favor doubling-down on a failing approach rather than try something new. If a strategy hasn't made a dent in crime for years, why persist? We have to be smarter with existing assets and more imaginative with strategy selection.

Back in 1994, policing scholar David Bayley wrote: "The police do not prevent crime. This is one of the best kept secrets of modern life. Experts know it, the police know it, but the public does not know it."[4] Fortunately, since then, police and crime scientists have examined a number of tactics and we have more knowledge on what works than when Bayley was writing over 20 years ago. Use the web pages suggested later in this chapter to select strategies that are more likely to succeed, and be prepared to vary your approach if you do not get the results you want. Build evaluation into your projects (with the PANDA process) so you can recognize when it's time to switch strategy.

Don't rely on outputs

There are certain mantras that everyone should live by, including 'no novelty neckties,' 'never get involved in a land war in Asia,' and 'oxfords, not brogues' (okay, admittedly those last two are from *The Princess Bride* and *Kingsman: The Secret Service*). To these we should add 'outcomes not outputs.'

Outputs are measures of how active police are. They include the number of drink-drive breath tests, arrests, pedestrian stops, and what not. Outputs aren't unimportant, because sometimes they provide reassurance to the community and demonstrate effort on behalf of the police service. But they aren't what the public cares ultimately about. The public cares about outcomes. Outcomes are the important measures that affect the community, such as burglary numbers, homicide rates, and public satisfaction. They demonstrate effectiveness at our core mission. If you have a burglary problem, setting an objective of increasing the number of burglary arrests (an output) or saturation

Figure 6.2 Inputs, outputs, and outcomes

patrols (another output) may not actually have any impact on the number of burglaries (the *outcome* most relevant to the problem).

The following are all examples of *outputs*, activities we might do to achieve our goals:

- the number of saturation patrols in a housing project
- an increase in the percentage of the public that saw foot patrols in the town center
- the number of bar door staff trained in de-escalation techniques.

These are all intermediate measures of activity (see Figure 6.2), but related and preferable *outcomes* might be:

- a reduction in burglaries at the housing project
- a reduction in the public's perceived fear of crime in the town center
- fewer reported assaults at town center bars and clubs.

Outcomes are why you joined the job. The objective of your operation or strategy should therefore be a relevant outcome. But outcomes are harder to achieve and not guaranteed, and they are often more difficult to measure. All of which makes them worthy of celebration when you can show meaningful success. In Figure 6.2 they are reliant on the effect of outputs, and those outputs have to be tied to a strong link to the outcomes you want to change.[5] In other words, the outputs will only work if they tap into the right mechanism (see next section on *Crime prevention* as well as Chapter 10 on Evidence-based policing). The bottom line is: don't rely on outputs, but instead make improving outcomes your mission.

Don't rely on your intuition

Cody Telep and Cynthia Lum asked over 900 police officers from three different departments what should be the balance between scientific knowledge and personal experience in day-to-day decision-making. Not surprisingly, they generally thought that their experience was more important than scientific knowledge.[6] I say not surprisingly, because until recently there hasn't been a strong movement to push ideas of evidence-based practice. Policing is still very much a craft learned through experience.

Recently I've been taking the survey a little farther. Like Telep and Lum, I ask: "What do you think should be the balance between the use of scientific research and personal experience in your day-to-day decision-making?" Then I go on to also ask about the best cop the officer knows. Every station has one. That one officer who seems to be able to spot a stolen car blindfold, or interview a belligerent suspect and have them eating out of their hand in 10 minutes. Generally, cops say that these 'natural police' should be allowed to use even more experience and intuition over scientific research (see Figure 6.3).

When asked about the least experienced, most accident-prone or generally unaware officer at the station, the responses are reversed— this officer's intuition shouldn't be let loose on the public! Instead, they should use evidence from the research on crime problems where available.

We recognize that officers can have a range of experience and intuition, and that this level of intuition should factor into decision-making. We also tend to think that *we* have the requisite intuition. But

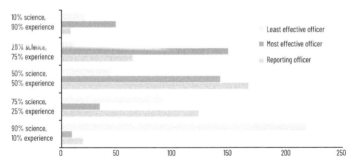

Figure 6.3 Science versus experience in decision-making

this assumption is rarely evaluated. My discussions with police leaders suggest that intuition is never a factor in promotion exams, yet most associate rank with experience and increased professional intuition.

Consider this medical study. Three highly-trained pathologists coded nearly 200 biopsies of patients with cancer and tried to predict the survival time of the patients.[7] These ratings were pretty poor—there was no correlation between predictions and outcomes. But the characteristics that the physicians used were found to have much better predictive value. In other words, the components that the doctors used were more useful than the specific judgments themselves.

This might translate to policing. There is evidence that police officers are not as good at identifying crime hot spots as a computer algorithm,[8] but they may have the experience to understand *why* the places are hot spots. And that expertise may be vital for figuring out a viable solution. Be open to learning more about what is going on, and integrating new information with your experience. Supplement your intuition with other forms of evidence (see Chapter 10).

With these caveats in place, we can now focus on what might be achievable.

CRIME PREVENTION

Prevention is the cornerstone of effective police efforts to combat crime and disorder. In policing, we can only do so much to alter the long-term motivations and moral filters of offenders, but we can reduce the opportunities that they exploit.

Removing the easier opportunities is so effective it even works when people are highly motivated. Take suicide for example. You read about the Bloor Street Viaduct in Toronto in the previous chapter. The British coal gas story is equally illustrative. When town gas, high in carbon monoxide, was available in every home in the U.K., a popular method of suicide was to put your head in an unlit oven with the gas left on. During the 1960s, the country's gas supply changed and the carbon monoxide level was reduced to non-fatal levels. Not only did suicides by gas oven disappear, but the total number of suicides in the country dropped as well. By removing the easy opportunity, a significant hurdle was placed in the way of people in temporary mental health distress.[9]

Crime prevention practitioners focus on 25 techniques with a strong focus on opportunity reduction.[10] They are grouped into five main prevention mechanisms. A prevention mechanism is a theory or idea about *how* an intervention will reduce or prevent a crime or disorder problem. It could:

- increase the effort of crime
- increase the risks of crime
- reduce the rewards of crime
- reduce provocations
- remove excuses.

These five mechanisms describe different avenues to reduce the opportunities that are available to offenders. Target hardening, controlling access to weapons, and screening facilities are all examples of increasing the effort (items 1–5 in Box 6.1). Increasing the risks requires a different tack. While improved street lighting and installing CCTV cameras on buses do not in themselves reduce the effort required to commit assault or other crimes, items 6–10 (again in Box 6.1) do increase the likelihood of getting caught. They increase the risks of engaging in crime.

Items 11–15 relate to reducing the rewards of crime. Apple Pay and other forms of cashless payment reduce the rewards of street robbery, and speed bumps reduce the enjoyment of speeding. Options 16–20 are suggested ways to reduce the provocations that can often trigger crime and anti-social behavior. Providing roped areas for people waiting in long lines can reduce their concerns about queue-jumpers, and having fixed fares (especially from airports) can avoid disputes with cab drivers. Finally, options 21–25 have some simple ideas to remove the excuses that offenders sometimes use to justify anti-social behavior. These include posting clear signs and providing ways for people to be more compliant with good behavior. In areas popular for drinking and entertainment, providing sufficient public lavatories is a good example.

BOX 6.1 THE 25 TECHNIQUES OF SITUATIONAL CRIME PREVENTION

Increase the effort	Increase the risks	Reduce the rewards	Reduce provocations	Remove excuses
1. Target harden Steering column locks and immobilizers Anti-robbery screens Tamper-proof packaging	**6. Extend guardianship** Take routine precautions: go out in group at night, leave signs of occupancy Campus night bus "Cocoon" neighborhood watch	**11. Conceal targets** Off-street parking Gender-neutral phone directories Unmarked bullion trucks	**16. Reduce frustrations and stress** Efficient queues and polite service Expanded seating Soothing music/muted lights	**21. Set rules** Rental agreements Harassment codes Hotel registration instructions
2. Control access to facilities Entry phones to buildings Electronic card access Baggage screening	**7. Assist natural surveillance** Improved street lighting Defensible space design Support whistleblowers	**12. Remove targets** Removable car entertainment Women's refuges Apply Pay and other non-cash options	**17. Avoid disputes** Separate enclosures for rival soccer fans Reduce crowding in pubs Fixed cab fares	**22. Post instructions** "No Parking" "Private Property" "Extinguish camp fires"

3. Screen exits	8. Reduce anonymity	13. Identify property	18. Reduce emotional arousal	23. Alert conscience
Ticket needed for exit	Taxi driver IDs	Property marking	Controls on violent pornography	Roadside speed display boards
Export documents	"How's my driving?" decals	Vehicle licensing and parts marking	Enforce good behavior on soccer field	Signatures for customs declarations
Electronic merchandise tags	School uniforms	Cattle branding	Prohibit racial slurs	"Shoplifting is stealing" signs
4. Deflect offenders	**9. Utilize place managers**	**14. Disrupt markets**	**19. Neutralize peer pressure**	**24. Assist compliance**
Street closures	CCTV for double-deck buses	Monitor pawn shops	"Idiots drink and drive"	Easy library checkout
Separate bathrooms for women	Two clerks for convenience stores	Controls on classified ads.	"It's OK to say No" campaigns	Public lavatories
Disperse pubs at closing time	Reward vigilance	License street vendors	Disperse troublemakers at school	Trash cans
5. Control tools/weapons	**10. Strengthen formal surveillance**	**15. Deny benefits**	**20. Discourage imitation**	**25. Control drugs and alcohol**
"Smart" guns	Red light cameras	Ink merchandise tags	Rapid repair of vandalism	Breathalyzers in pubs
Disabling stolen cell phones	Burglar alarms	Graffiti cleaning	V-chips in TVs	Server intervention
Restrict spray paint sales to juveniles	Security guards	Speed humps	Censor details of modus operandi	Alcohol-free events

The key to using Box 6.1 effectively is to have a thorough understanding of the problem. This returns us back to your VOLTAGE checklist in Chapter 4. The way that some of the techniques identified in

BOX 6.2 FIXING MARGARET RIVER'S WICKED PROBLEM

"My first significant command was in a tourist town in the heart of wine country. Everyone was either producing or consuming the stuff so alcohol-related crime was high. Other government agencies were a two hour drive away, so they were little help. I had my work cut out for me, and I wasn't really prepared for it.

We had a real issue with one tavern. People would leave and walk quarter of a mile to the local kebab shop. They had their 'doof doof' music playing round the back of a carpark in the dark. A perfect location to continue with the party! We were continually called for serious assaults, disturbances, and, in the morning, complaints from local businesses about the urine, empty bottles, and so on. The mentality from local politicians and citizens was: 'Why haven't you locked anyone up? That's the only way we're going to stop it. Let them know you are not going to tolerate this type of behavior.' I knew this wouldn't work in the long term so had to change that mindset to one of 'how do we stop it from occurring in the first place?'

I obtained a grant, and got timed lighting and CCTV installed. The kebab store owners didn't want to lose business but I explained a safe environment was going to bring more people, not less. The changes have withstood the test of time, and the issue that was once the talking point of the town, became history."

Paul Daly is a senior sergeant with the Western Australia Police Force and is currently a project manager assigned to the policing innovation and improvement team.

Box 6.1 work are subtly different and require a nuanced appreciation for the dynamics of the crime problem. Sometimes there is pressure for an enforcement solution, but as Paul Daly explains in Box 6.2, prevention may require more effort but it leads to a longer-term solution.

If you are not sure what approach might work, you could consider trying two different mechanisms in different places and then test to find out which is more effective. You could employ different techniques that function over different time periods. For example, implementing a camera surveillance system can take months to set up and organize. A second tactic that can help temporarily in the short term until the cameras are installed might be fruitful. You could, for example, choose an enforcement approach for short-term relief, and a prevention tactic for longer-term crime prevention.

Your colleagues may have ideas that are not covered by the examples in Box 6.1. When evaluating their idea, an ideal approach to ask yourself is "What is the mechanism that would make this work?" In other words, how will it change a component of the crime triangle such that the opportunity for crime will be different?

ENFORCEMENT

The E in your VIPER checklist is Enforcement (see Chapter 7). Enforcement is the bread-and-butter of many police departments, and often the default choice for many commanders faced with crime problems. Enforcement can cover a range of operational tactics and common options include:

• saturation patrol of an area with uniform resources
• a crackdown on drug dealers with undercover officers or narcotics units
• drink-drive (DUI) checkpoints in traffic accident black spots.

Enforcement benefits and negatives

Use of patrol and related assets has a number of benefits. They are a resource that can be quickly dispatched to address an emerging crime panic. This can demonstrate to senior executives and the community that 'something is being done'. Enforcement can also be an effective tool to send a signal to the offending community, and has been shown to work in crime hot spots (see later section on crime hot spots in this chapter).

While enforcement might reduce a problem in the short-term, this can too easily become a long-term, open-ended commitment.

In general, enforcement can provide a short-term respite from a crime problem, though it is sometimes difficult to discern if the relief comes from police work or from a regression to the mean (see Box 3.6 on page 45). Enforcement is a tactic police can do immediately, without having to coordinate with community partners or other government agencies.

These benefits aside, enforcement rarely, if ever, addresses the underlying cause of a problem. When Paul Daly tackled his troublesome bar and shop in Margaret River (see Box 6.2), he recognized the futility of an extended enforcement approach. If you have a lone wolf that is a recidivist residential burglar in your area then making an arrest may solve the problem. I once arrested a fearless burglar who climbed onto the roof of a tower block and swung himself over the building edge onto the balcony of an apartment. While my colleagues rushed to the top floor apartment, I stayed outside and watched him climb down ten floors of the building, swinging precariously from balcony to balcony in spectacular fashion. I hid behind a tree and nicked him when he finally made it to the ground, exhausted. I almost felt sorry for him. In most cases, however, we quickly learn that it's difficult to arrest our way out of a problem. Because enforcement doesn't address whatever is the underlying issue (such as chronically insecure houses), inevitably more offenders will exploit the weakness.

While enforcement might reduce a problem in the short term, this can too easily become a long-term, open-ended commitment. The community becomes accustomed to a substantial police presence and this can reduce their interest in supporting other prevention approaches. Without a prevention solution alongside the enforcement, the quick fix becomes a drain on personnel and limits your ability to use enforcement as a stop-gap measure elsewhere.

Shift ownership of the problem

Crime sometimes occurs because some agency or corporate body fails to conduct its business in a way that prevents crime. In other words, they either intentionally or inadvertently cause crime by the way they operate. These agencies can sometimes be encouraged, or if necessary coerced, into reforming their ways. By shifting responsibility onto the business that owns the problem, you can free up officers to focus elsewhere.

This might, however, require some work on your part. For example, some businesses are too cheap to implement necessary prevention, or may even profit from crime. They may have procedures that inhibit good crime solutions, or simply be ignorant that they can do something about it. They may not even agree it is their problem. You can draw on a range of options that have increasing levels of coercion and effort to get the problem owner to take responsibility. These were developed by Herman Goldstein as a hierarchy of approaches that start benignly for agencies that are willing to cooperate with you, and move to more punitive solutions if they are less cooperative (see Box 6.3).

The Union of European Football Associations (UEFA) takes this approach. UEFA's Control, Ethics and Disciplinary Body (CEDB) deals with disciplinary cases, both on and off the field. When fans misbehave in significant ways, such as violence, pitch invasions, racist chants, or throwing fireworks and other objects, the CEDB can take action against the football club. They are able to fine the teams, ban them from selling tickets for games, suspend players or coaches, and even enforce the closure of various stands from where fans watch games. Instead of trying to prosecute unruly fans directly, the CEDB shifts responsibility for policing the fans onto the clubs.

BOX 6.3 SHIFTING RESPONSIBILITY TO PROBLEM OWNERS

Cooperation level	Implementation difficulty	Mechanism
Least	Most	Bring a civil action
		Legislation mandating adoption of prevention
		Charge a fee for police service
		Withdraw police service
		Public shaming
		Creation of a new organization to assume ownership
		Engage another existing organization
		Targeted confrontational requests
		Straightforward informal requests
Most	Least	Educational programs

Shifting the responsibility back onto the owner of the problem can be time-consuming and sometimes challenging legally and politically. As you go up the hierarchy in Box 6.3, it definitely becomes more difficult and coercive. But if you don't take on these challenges, you will be continually spending the public's money and wasting your limited resources.

HOT SPOTS POLICING

'Early-turn' at Bow Road in London's East End had a comforting routine to it. The 6 am roll-call (as it is called in the U.S.) involved the sergeant reading out the latest news from the 'parade book' and assigned everyone to various vehicles or foot beats. Then we shuffled off to the canteen for a cup of tea together (prepared in advance by the youngest member of the relief) before heading out to save humanity from itself. We were dispatched across the district to cover as much territory as possible with random patrol.

We didn't know any better at the time, but the evidence is now clear that random patrol doesn't reduce crime. Innovative departments are starting to move away from assignment to pre-determined sectors and are posting officers to known crime hot spots, a strategy that is more effective. Most jurisdictions have places where crime is frequent enough that it is fairly predictable, at least over longer periods of time (chronic problem places). Most officers quickly learn where crime hot spots are located in their jurisdiction, though software programs and crime analysts can improve our understanding of these crime problems.

There isn't really a standard definition of a place for hot spots policing, but in general crime hot spots are places as small as individual buildings or street corners, blocks or clusters of a few streets, where crime is higher relative to the rest of the area. The term is generally not used once you get to the size of whole neighborhoods. The criminological explanations for why crime hot spots exist were discussed in the previous chapter: the opportunity theories, and crime attractors and crime generators.

The mechanism by which most hot spots policing works is deterrence. Hot spots policing strategies increase police attention to places with concentrated criminal opportunities. Additional attention or increased enforcement can convey a heightened sense of risk of apprehension to potential offenders. This discourages the crooks from taking advantage of opportunities (though note that it doesn't change the distribution of opportunities).

Hot spots policing relies primarily on focused law enforcement strategies. There is no standardized list of hot spot approaches and various tactics have been applied in recent years. Successful approaches have in the past included increased gun searches and seizures,[11] foot patrols,[12] problem-oriented policing,[13] and offender-focused tactics.[14] In a summary of a number of randomized trials, Anthony Braga and his colleagues found that hot spots policing has a positive effect on crime, but was more effective with problem-oriented policing rather than more traditional tactics.[15]

In 2004 the National Research Council (U.S.) concluded that "studies that focused police resources on crime hot spots provide the strongest collective evidence of police effectiveness that is now available."[16] The recent National Academies of Sciences, Engineering, and Medicine panel on proactive policing also concluded "hot spots policing interventions generate statistically significant crime reduction impacts without simply displacing crime into areas immediately surrounding the targeted locations."[17] Results differ depending on the crime problem, with less benefits for disorder offenses and more for drug crime.[15] There also tends to be a diffusion of benefits to nearby areas. The number of studies in this area is still limited, but in general, hot spots policing has the potential to reduce crime by statistically significant amounts.

> *In general, hot spots policing has the potential to reduce crime by statistically significant amounts.*

While designed for foot patrol areas,[18] the general principles here can be adapted for many crime hot spots:

- If the local mail carrier does not walk, then the area may not be suited for a focused patrol unless you have mobile units such as bicycles.
- Smaller beats encompassing only a few streets appear to be more effective than larger areas that dilute any positive effects.
- Adjust hot spot areas after they have been operational for a time to avoid a decay in the enthusiasm of officers to engage in activity, or to prevent offenders getting to know the officers' patrol patterns.
- Maximize efficiency by deploying via the specific geography and timing of the problem, rather than the convenience of shift times. This prevents the Roman Road Market problem I encountered and explained at the start of Chapter 4.

PROACTIVE STRATEGIES

The U.S. National Academies of Sciences, Engineering, and Medicine define proactive policing as "all policing strategies that have as one of their goals the prevention or reduction of crime and disorder and that are not reactive in terms of focusing primarily on uncovering ongoing crime or on investigating or responding to crimes once they have occurred."[17] Proactive policing strategies are predominantly police-driven and target activities towards certain places or people. By focusing police investigation on specific individuals or groups, they convey an increased perceived risk of police interdiction should offending occur.

> Proactive policing strategies are predominantly police-driven and target activities towards certain places or people. By focusing police investigation on specific individuals or groups, they convey an increased perceived risk of police interdiction should offending occur.

The report made the point that while individual officers can choose to be proactive in particular circumstances, a proactive policing strategy is where you make a decision "to use proactive police responses in a programmatic way to reduce crime." There are four main approaches to proactive policing, with different logic models, strategies, and ways they accomplish their goals (see Table 6.1).

Six percent of the population commit 60 percent of the crime. The potential is therefore significant. While at the time of writing the evidence around offender-targeted strategies is still fairly limited, there are some studies that can inform your strategies.

For example, during the Philadelphia Policing Tactics Experiment, officers who worked in offender-focus areas engaged with serious, repeat offenders in a variety of ways.[14] Working from lists provided by their colleagues and officers from the criminal intelligence unit,

Table 6.1 Four approaches to proactive policing

	Place-based	Problem-solving	Person-focused	Community-based
Logic model	Capitalize on the evidence for the concentration of crime at micro places	Use a problem-solving approach to identify the causes for patterns of events, and tailor solutions to them	Capitalize on the strong concentration of crime among a small proportion of the criminal population	Capitalize on the resources of communities to identify and control crime
Policing strategies	Hot spots policing; predictive policing; CCTV	Problem-oriented policing; third party policing; proactive partnering	Focused deterrence; repeat offender programs; stop, question, and frisk	Community-oriented policing; procedural justice policing; broken windows policing
Primary objective	Prevent crime in micro-geographic areas	Solve recurring problems to prevent future crime	Prevent and deter specific crimes by targeting known offenders	Enhance collective efficacy and community collaboration with police
Key ways to accomplish objective	Identification of crime hot spots and application of focused strategies	Scan and analyze crime problems, and identify solutions	Identify known high-rate offenders and apply strategies to them	Develop approaches that engage the community, or change how police interact with citizens

Source: Adapted from Weisburd, D., & Majmundar, M. K. (Eds.). (2017). *Proactive Policing: Effects on Crime and Communities.* Washington, DC: National Academies of Sciences (Consensus Study Report).

they made frequent contact with local offenders, including small talk, serving arrest warrants, and conducting surveillance. The identities of the targeted offenders were widely distributed around the districts. Compared to equivalent control areas, violence reduced by 42 percent, and serious violent felonies were cut in half. Surveys of people in the crime hot spots before and after the experiment found that while folk didn't feel much safer, at least they did not feel crime was worse and there was no evidence of 'backfire effects' where there is a loss of police legitimacy (see summary in Box 10.4 on page 196).[19]

That being said, proactive policing can be considered uninvited and potentially intrusive into the lives of specific offenders or can focus police resources in a place such that there is an impact on residents' daily activities. Proportionality and common sense in the application of enforcement are therefore important. The evaluation of offender-focused policing strategies is still in its relative infancy, but many agencies are starting to look at this promising approach (see Box 6.4).

Six percent of the population commit 60 percent of the crime.

BOX 6.4 TARGETING OFFENDER-FOCUSED PATROL TIME

"As the director of our agency's intelligence-led policing section, I had the tough task of trying to change a culture, which everyone in law enforcement knows isn't easy. We train our deputies to be better consumers of intelligence products and encourage them to use these to drive their enforcement actions.

For example, many deputies enjoy spending their unallocated patrol time running traffic, but we push for deputies to have self-initiated activity that is targeted, offender-focused, and guided by the products from our analysts. Through the use of social network analysis, we highlight key impact offenders who are the most influential within their networks and whose apprehension will net the greatest impact to our crime environment.

This change in focus has helped us reduce burglaries 38 percent over the last three years, significantly outpacing the state and country. Furthermore, we try to convey to commanders the need to be consistently innovative. Even when you find an initiative works, start developing the next. Don't wait for it to become stale. That is how we keep the criminals guessing, and how we stop responding to crime and start preventing crime."

Justin Ross is currently a captain over the operational readiness division for the Pasco County Sheriff's Office in Florida (U.S.). He previously served as the director of their intelligence-led policing section.

Focused deterrence strategies

Many police services struggle with gang problems. When offenders join a gang, it is usually the case that their offending increases in frequency and seriousness, and their criminal careers last longer. Gang areas have increased levels of gun assaults and when the gang uses their area for drug dealing, property and violence levels are higher than in non-gang areas.[20] While gang take-downs can be common, few have been properly evaluated. As a result, the long-term impact of these crackdowns is not well understood. By contrast, there has been considerable effort to examine the outcomes from focused deterrence strategies.

Focused deterrence increases the certainty, swiftness, and severity of police interdiction and punishment, by communicating the consequences directly to offenders while also providing motivations to desist from crime. Use of these strategies has increased in popularity in recent years. These are person-focused approaches where police or prosecutors make direct contact with high-risk offenders. It is an "attempt to transform a vague and generalized threat of arrest into an explicit, personalized, and highly salient warning that arrest is imminent if the individuals persist in offending."[17] This approach is sometimes called a pulling levers strategy.

The first evaluation was the Boston Operation Ceasefire program in the 1990s. The program's suppression mechanisms included aggressive use of probation restrictions, tapping into expansive federal enforcement options, and pursuit of warrants and long sentences. With the aid of other officers, the project could also disrupt street drug activity, or target low-level street crimes such as public drinking. At the same time, social service providers, as well as the gang members' probation and parole officers, offered various services and other ways to help the gang members move away from their violent lifestyle. These support messages were reinforced by the local communities and churches. The program resulted in a decrease in youth homicides, citywide gun assaults, and calls for service.[21]

A number of other focused deterrence approaches that share characteristics with the original Boston work have been found to be promising. The Group Violence Reduction Strategy in New Orleans (Louisiana, U.S.) reduced the homicide rate by 17 percent compared to comparable cities.[22] In Chicago (Illinois, U.S.) Cure Violence chose to deploy trained street violence interrupters and outreach workers. They also used public education campaigns, and a similar style of community mobilization. These efforts resulted in significant reductions in shootings of between 17 and 24 percent, and reductions in retaliatory homicides.[23]

Focused deterrence takes a considerable amount of coordination and agreement between different police and government agencies, community groups, and non-government partners. Braga and Weisburd[24] summarize their review with these policy implications:

- tailor partnerships and tactics to address underlying conditions
- heighten the perceived risk of apprehension
- decrease opportunity structures for crime

- deflect offenders from crime with services such as employment or substance abuse assistance
- increase community collective efficacy by engaging family members and the community
- improve the legitimacy of police actions.

Senior leaders reading this should be aware that the research strongly suggests that focused deterrence strategies appear to work best when adapted to local conditions and specific neighborhood contexts. Area commanders and their officers are usually in the best place to know the local context and to tailor workable solutions and partnerships.

Sometimes, these more coordinated approaches are not possible or are difficult to organize between partner agencies. When combined with hot spots policing or at least confined to specific neighborhoods or gang areas, police only interventions can still be effective. Examples include an operation launched against a drug gang in Brightwood, Indianapolis (U.S.)[25] and Operation Thumbs Down, an FBI-led gang take-down in South Central Los Angeles (described in Chapter 9). When police in Liverpool (U.K.) arranged for court-ordered two-year injunctions against three dozen gang members, more than 90 percent of the gang members reduced their offending. They were also less likely to be a victim of crime.[26]

CHAPTER SUMMARY

- The limitations of the criminal justice system are significant enough that there is little evidence that general arrest and prosecution strategies can impact on crime.
- Don't rely on outputs, but instead make improving outcomes your objective.
- Don't rely on your intuition, but instead supplement it with other evidence (see Chapter 10).
- Use the techniques for situational crime prevention and focus on increasing the effort of crime, increasing the risks, reducing the rewards, reducing provocations, and removing excuses.

- Consider indirect enforcement that shifts ownership of the problem.
- Hot spots policing in high crime areas has been shown to be an effective policing strategy.
- Numerous focused deterrence approaches have been shown to be effective at reducing violence.

REFERENCES

1 Maple, J. and C. Mitchell, *The Crime Fighter: Putting the Bad Guys out of Business.* 1999, New York: Doubleday.

2 Ratcliffe, J.H., *Intelligence-Led Policing (2nd edition)*. 2016, Abingdon, Oxon.: Routledge.

3 Weisburd, D. and J. Eck, *What can police do to reduce crime, disorder, and fear?* The Annals of the American Academy of Political and Social Science, 2004. **593**(1): p. 43–65.

4 Bayley, D.H., *Police for the Future.* 1994, New York: Oxford University Press.

5 Spottiswoode, C., *Improving Police Performance: A New Approach to Measuring Police Efficiency: Technical Annexes.* 2000, London: Public Services Productivity Panel.

6 Telep, C.W. and C. Lum, *The receptivity of officers to empirical research and evidence-based policing: An examination of survey data from three agencies.* Police Quarterly, 2014. **17**(4): p. 359–85.

7 Einhorn, H.J., *Expert measurement and mechanical combination.* Organizational Behavior & Human Performance, 1972. **7**(1): p. 86–106.

8 Macbeth, E. and B. Ariel, *Place-based statistical versus clinical predictions of crime hot spots and harm locations in Northern Ireland.* Justice Quarterly, 2017: p. 1–34.

9 Kreitman, N., *The coal gas story. United Kingdom suicide rates, 1960–71.* British Journal of Preventive & Social Medicine, 1976. **30**(2): p. 86–93.

10 Clarke, R.V., *Situational crime prevention, in Environmental Criminology and Crime Analysis*, R. Wortley and L. Mazerolle, Editors. 2008, Willan Publishing: Cullompton, Devon. p. 178–94.

11 Sherman, L.W., J.W. Shaw, and D.P. Rogan, *The Kansas City Gun Experiment.* 1995, Washington DC: National Institute of Justice. p. 11.

12 Ratcliffe, J.H., et al., *The Philadelphia Foot Patrol Experiment: A randomized controlled trial of police patrol effectiveness in violent crime hotspots.* Criminology, 2011. **49**(3): p. 795–831.

13 Braga, A.A. and B.J. Bond, *Policing crime and disorder hot spots: A randomized controlled trial.* Criminology, 2008. **46**(3): p. 577–607.

14 Groff, E.R., et al., *Does what police do at hot spots matter? The Philadelphia Policing Tactics Experiment.* Criminology, 2015. **51**(1): p. 23–53.

15 Braga, A.A., A.V. Papachristos, and D.M. Hureau, *The effects of hot spots policing on crime: An updated systematic review and meta-analysis.* Justice Quarterly, 2014. **31**(4): p. 633–63.

16 National Research Council, *Fairness and Effectiveness in Policing: The Evidence.* 2004, Committee to Law and Justice, Division of Behavioral and Social Sciences and Education: Washington, D.C.

17 Weisburd, D. and M.K. Majmundar, eds. *Proactive Policing: Effects on Crime and Communities.* 2017, National Academies of Sciences Consensus Study Report: Washington, D.C.

18 Ratcliffe, J.H. and E.T. Sorg, *Foot Patrol: Rethinking the Cornerstone of Policing.* 2017, New York: Springer (CriminologyBriefs).

19 Ratcliffe, J.H., et al., *Citizens' reactions to hot spots policing: Impacts on perceptions of crime, disorder, safety and police.* Journal of Experimental Criminology, 2015. **11**(3): p. 393–417.

20 Ratcliffe, J.H., A. Perenzin, and E.T. Sorg, *Operation Thumbs Down: A quasi-experimental evaluation of an FBI gang takedown in South Central Los Angeles.* Policing: An International Journal of Police Strategies and Management, 2017. **40**(2): p. 442–58.

21 Braga, A.A., et al., *Problem-oriented policing, deterrence, and youth violence: An evaluation of Boston's Operation Ceasefire.* Journal of Research in Crime and Delinquency, 2001. **38**(3): p. 195–225.

22 Corsaro, N. and R.S. Engel, *Most challenging of contexts.* Criminology and Public Policy, 2015. **14**(3): p. 471–505.

23 Skogan, W.G., et al., *Evaluation of CeaseFire-Chicago.* 2009, National Institute of Justice: Washington, D.C.

24 Braga, A.A. and D.L. Weisburd, *Pulling levers focused deterrence strategies to prevent crime,* in *Crime Prevention Research Review No. 6.* 2012, Office of Community Oriented Policing Services: Washington, D.C.

25 Nunn, S., et al., *Interdiction Day: Covert surveillance operations, drugs, and serious crime in an inner-city neighborhood.* Police Quarterly, 2006. **9**(1): p. 73–99.

26 Carr, R., M. Slothower, and J. Parkinson, *Do gang injunctions reduce violent crime? Four tests in Merseyside, UK.* Cambridge Journal of Evidence-Based Policing, 2017.

7

NOMINATING YOUR STRATEGY

DEFINE YOUR MISSION STATEMENT

When I served at Bow Road Police Station, we had a small blue poster in a slightly askew and faded frame in the canteen. It was quite incongruous there on the wall by itself. I was probably the only person ever to glance at the poster. It contained the mission statement of the police service, no doubt developed with expensive consultants and many focus groups. You have probably walked past one every day and rarely given it any thought. Nobody can ever recite the content's noble statements but they tend to contain some inspirational yet vague declarations. Are there any police departments that *don't* want to enhance public safety?

For your crime reduction strategy, you need something more specific. Your mission statement is a clear and unambiguous declaration about the outcome or outcomes you want to change. It should relate to a crime, disorder, or harm outcome that you identified in your problem scan, and not an output. Now that you have completed the P and A of PANDA, and have a background in opportunity theories and how police can impact on crime, your mission statement leads into nominating your strategy.

A variation of a litmus test I use for project evaluation might help here.[1] Imagine that you have already designed your operation. Now complete this sentence: "The operation aims to make the community safer with (i) _____ (ii) _____."

Examples of what you might write for (i) and (ii) are:

- (i) "a significant increase in" (ii) "public perception of safety in the high street"
- (i) "a substantial cut in the" (ii) "assault complaints at Willie's nightclub"
- (i) "a 10% reduction in" (ii) "reported street crime."

You might have guessed that (i) is an indication of a change that you want to create, and (ii) is the all-important outcome that is the community concern. Some caution is warranted with the last example. You might think being specific with a percentage goal demonstrates strong leadership through the setting of ambitious targets; however, it can also pressure officers and more junior commanders to game the statistics and reclassify crimes incorrectly. These mission statements should therefore be seen as focused aims rather than targets. You may have nothing but honorable intentions, but people underneath you might interpret these targets as an 'or-else' mandate and when under pressure respond in a less-than-ethical fashion.

You can choose to have more than one mission with an operation. You might want to reduce a particular crime problem as well as develop and sustain levels of public confidence. If so, you should state these, but also be cautious as you move forward. The contributions of different activities work in different ways and need to be weighed and balanced against all of your mission goals.

With this in place, you can now nominate your strategy for achieving the outcomes, using VIPER. You will build on your mission statement as you go through the VIPER-related outcomes. It will also be helpful to read this chapter in conjunction with Chapter 10, and especially Table 10.2 which explains how to build evidence into decision-making.

NOMINATING A VIPER STRATEGY

The N in PANDA is *Nominate strategy* (or also *Nominate*). Here we focus on the VIPER checklist as a structure for not only a range of enforcement and prevention options, but also to help you to think through other strategy items such as reassurance, victim support, and gathering criminal intelligence. Some police services have in the past recommended a PIER framework but given the growing importance of victim support over the last few years, the V component has been added to make this checklist VIPER (see Box 7.1).

You should at least consider all five items, even if you decide you may not be able to do every one of them. There is always value in keeping an open mind about different approaches and perhaps combining styles of operation strategy. In some cases, you might conduct multiple activities under one of the VIPER items. Give each VIPER item some consideration.

Each VIPER item can be linked to your mission statement by a mechanism. Remember that a prevention mechanism is a theory or idea about how an intervention will reduce a crime or disorder problem. For example, if you decide that an enforcement (E in VIPER) approach is to conduct frequent bar checks in an entertainment area plagued with drunken fights, you might do this because it will remove the bar owners' excuses and encourage them to be more responsible about not serving clearly intoxicated patrons. This is the mechanism you think will drive the change you want to see. It is useful to link your prevention and enforcement VIPER responses

---

BOX 7.1 THE VIPER CHECKLIST

Victim support
Intelligence gaps
Prevention
Enforcement
Reassurance

to one of the five main mechanisms described in detail in Chapter 6 and along the top of Box 6.1, namely:

- increase the effort of crime
- increase the risks of crime
- reduce the rewards of crime
- reduce provocations
- remove excuses.

You can add this to your mission statement. For example, if your statement reads "This operation aims to make the community safer with (i) a 20% reduction in (ii) residential burglary at the Waramanga public housing project" then you can add a third and fourth element: "The enforcement strategy of (iii) _____ will achieve this by (iv) _____."

Examples of what you might write for (iii) and (iv) are dependent on your strategy, but you can draw on the five crime prevention mechanisms as a starting point for (iv). A complete mission statement with example VIPER responses can be found later in the chapter in Box 7.8. First, let's look at how to build your VIPER responses.

Victim support (V)

The V in your VIPER checklist is *Victim support*. Victims are the people who are harmed by a crime or other wrong. The harm may be physical but it can also be emotional. Crime can also affect family members and other people who were not necessarily the target of crime directly. It is easy to become a little numb to the experiences of victims when you have been in policing a long time just by dint of having reported a lot of crime over the years. Victims of crime are likely to feel shocked, humiliated, or intimidated by the experience. They may even be traumatized, which can compound difficulties if they are also necessary to an investigation as a witness. Reminding your officers that for each victim it might be their first time is an important component of victim support.

When treated with empathy, respect, and sensitivity, crime victims are more likely to cooperate with crime investigations, listen to crime prevention advice, and report positive perceptions of trust and confidence in the police. This is part of the notion of procedural justice, an important concept that is discussed in greater detail in the final chapter (the components are also summarized later in Box 11.4).

Better relationships with crime victims, victims' advocacy groups, and victim service providers can improve organizational reputation and morale. Perhaps most importantly from an area commander's perspective is the realization that projects that have specifically addressed repeat victimization have successfully reduced crime.[2]

As a starting point (if your department doesn't do this already) a general policy of support for victims is necessary. You can draft a policy that addresses the seven critical areas that the International Association of Chiefs of Police argue are where victims may need support and assistance[3] (see Box 7.2).

BOX 7.2 CRITICAL AREAS OF VICTIM SUPPORT

Safety	Protection from perpetrators and assistance in avoiding re-victimization
Support	Assistance to enable participation in justice system processes and repair of harm
Information	Concise and useful information about justice system processes and victim services
Access	Opportunity to participate in justice system processes and obtain information and services
Continuity	Consistency in approaches and methods across agencies through all stages of the justice process
Voice	Opportunities to speak out on specific case processing issues and larger policy questions
Justice	Receiving the support necessary to heal and seeing that perpetrators are held accountable for their actions

Beyond this uniform position on victim support, you may also need to determine a problem-specific response. Your support to a victim who had their car broken into with little stolen is likely to be different than dealing with a victim of chronic child abuse or sex trafficking. Depending on the particular problem you may, prior to deploying any strategy, need to:

- ensure that officers specially trained in (for example) domestic abuse or trafficking are available
- provide training or guidance to all officers likely to interact with victims
- nominate a coordinating officer who will liaise with victim support groups
- synchronize with prosecutors or outside agencies in advance of any cases
- coordinate with detectives to manage evidence capture with sensitivity and sense
- assign an intelligence contact to collate and assess any information gathered
- keep neighborhood and patrol teams appraised of any operations
- nominate someone to be responsible for ongoing victim support
- consider welfare support to officers affected by dealing with sensitive problems.

Each problem area will likely merit a tailored solution and it is not possible to list all of the necessary responses here. Check the accompanying website for additional resources.

Intelligence gaps (I)

The I in your VIPER checklist relates to *intelligence gaps*. Intelligence gaps are pieces of information that are currently 'known unknowns,' but when acquired can enhance your knowledge and possibly lead to a better operational decision. By including intelligence gaps in the VIPER checklist, you have an opportunity to learn from every operation, regardless of the outcome. Even if crime and disorder are not reduced at your first attempt, intelligence gained can inform the next operation, so at least this way your efforts will not be wasted.

Intelligence gaps can be identified by reviewing your VOLTAGE analysis. There are often some items that don't have much useful information available. For example, crime analysts are often good at completing details of crime locations (L) and times (T) but may know less about other components. These are your intelligence gaps.

You can sometimes task enforcement units with filling these gaps, if you promote the importance of collecting detailed and specific information. For example, plain-clothes officers can identify drivers of particular suspect vehicles, and you might remember that Kelly Robbins asked foot patrol officers to complete community burglary surveys (see Box 4.6 on page 68). Her surveys highlighted important modus operandi details that were not contained in the original crime reports. Filling intelligence gaps is achieved in a number of stages.

1 Review your VOLTAGE analysis to determine intelligence gaps.
2 Design a number of relatively simple intelligence requirements to fill the gaps.
3 Evaluate what resources you can deploy and are appropriate to complete the intelligence requirements.
4 Allocate specific requirements to particular units or individuals.
5 Assign an individual (perhaps yourself) to receive and review all information received.

Prevention (P)

Prevention is the cornerstone of modern law enforcement philosophy. This was recognized from the beginning of modern policing when Sir Richard Mayne wrote "The primary object of an efficient police is the prevention of crime: the next that of detection and punishment of offenders if crime is committed. To these ends all the efforts of police must be directed."[4]

One way that I like to challenge people in my training courses is to ask them: "If you had no police or enforcement resources that you could deploy, how could you reduce the problem?" This thought exercise gets the brain thinking about more imaginative solutions. For help, review Box 6.1 and the 25 techniques of crime prevention. The advantage of many of the ideas in Box 6.1 is that they do not incur a significant policing cost. The disadvantage is that they can take time to initiate. Because of this, an enforcement option that complements the prevention choice can be beneficial.

The major prevention suggestions have been covered in Chapter 6 so please refer to that chapter. Also refer to Chapter 10, and especially Table 10.2, which explains how to build evidence into decision-making. As you should aim to include at least one tactic from each of the VIPER elements, it is preferable to avoid an enforcement solution that you label as prevention. For example, it might be easy to assign saturation patrols to a crime hot spot and call this your prevention activity, but they could also be your enforcement option. As a result, they are not necessarily two different tactics.

If you had no police or enforcement resources that you could deploy, how could you reduce the problem?

Enforcement (E)

Enforcement activities are the bread-and-butter of many departments, though they can come with a significant cost in terms of police legitimacy and public trust if not conducted in a targeted and thoughtful manner. Some countries in Central America are still reeling from the aftermath of their indiscriminate use of police enforcement against gang members in the early part of this century (see Box 7.3).

> ## BOX 7.3 *MANO DURA* IN EL SALVADOR
>
> In a desperate attempt to control rampant gang violence, El Salvador adopted a policy of *Mano Dura* ('Iron Fist') initiated in July 2003 by Salvadoran President Francisco Flores. The policy promoted the immediate imprisonment of a gang member or suspected gang member for something as simple as having gang-related tattoos or being seen to flash gang signs in public. These offences became punishable with a jail sentence of up to five years and were applicable to suspected gang members as young as twelve years' old. By placing members into exclusive prisons for each gang, the government inadvertently strengthened gang command structures. While 20,000 gang members were arrested between July 2003 and August 2004, 95 percent were eventually released without charge.[5] The Salvadorian Supreme Court ultimately ruled the program unconstitutional. Many Salvadorian police officers privately blame *Mano Dura* for exacerbating the gang problem over time rather than reducing it.

The main enforcement discussion in this book has been covered in Chapter 6. But it is worth remembering that enforcement is often a short-term, stop-gap measure that can become a significant resource drain that doesn't address the underlying problem. Once you deploy officers to an area, the community become accustomed to seeing those officers and are resistant to their removal or redeployment. This can limit your future tactical options by reducing your resource flexibility.

Reassurance (R)

Reassurance is important given the gulf between fear of crime and actual crime (see the related Figure 1.1 in the opening chapter). People can worry about their safety so much that it affects their behavior. Programs that reassure the public through visibility, accessibility, and familiarity with local police may be necessary given that public perception of crime is frequently at odds with falling crime rates (a reassurance gap).[6, 7] The reassurance policing model, popular in the U.K., grew from this realization.

Some of the blame was felt to lie at the hands of signal crimes. This perspective suggests that the public's fear of being a victim of crime is not tied to aggregate data or statistics, but instead to certain 'signal' crimes or deviant acts that breach not only criminal law but also our conventions about social order.[8] These could either be dramatic and heavily publicized heinous acts, or the day-to-day background noise of wearisome disorder. In other words, signal crimes can be crime panics, crime spikes, or chronic problems (review Chapter 3). These signal crimes affect how people interpret their sense of risk and safety, and change their behavior. In some regards, part of the challenge for law enforcement is that much successful police work takes place away from public view. Too few people directly witness the successful arrests in dawn raids or late-night surveillance operations.

An individual's sense of insecurity stems from a number of items, four of which are within the control of police actions to some degree,[7] being:

- crime
- physical disorder
- social disorder
- social control.

In the U.K., the National Reassurance Policing Programme targeted policing activity and problem-solving to tackle crimes and disorder, community involvement in the process of identifying priorities and taking action to tackle them, and the presence of visible, accessible, and locally known officers in neighborhoods. These involved more than just community meetings and 'coffee with a cop.' They expanded to include street briefings, door knocking, and 'have a say days.'[9]

The majority of the test sites experienced reductions in crime and perceptions of anti-social behavior. They also increased the public's confidence in police, feelings of safety, and sense of trust in the local area. While reassurance policing has been criticized as 'there, there policing' or 'big hug policing,'[10] the evidence is clear that there is a reassurance gap. Any activities you can undertake to provide reassurance to the public, especially during well-publicized crime spikes, will likely be appreciated and will bolster public support for other operations.

It might seem like considerable effort to seek out a range of solutions from victim support to reassurance. After all, it is certainly easier to do just one tactic. But various strategies might be necessary to help build support and 'community restoration' (see Box 7.4).

BOX 7.4 BEYOND ENFORCEMENT TO ADDRESS COMMUNITY NEEDS

"On promotion I was assigned to one of Arlington's most challenged districts. There is always an integration process with a new assignment, as training doesn't always equate to experience. Many officers on the shift had more tenure as I had promoted rather quickly through the ranks. My leadership approach was to establish goals for the shift and work through my supervisors to get tasks accomplished. Not everyone will agree with your leadership philosophy, but you have to make decisions with the community, police, and government in mind.

I saw that a primary factor in our violent crime related to minority juveniles. Although we had mechanisms to work with youth, I thought we could better meet their needs. I started a mentoring program to fill gaps in community restoration, providing support, trust, and reassurance, and creating partnerships with youths and their parents. We increased police legitimacy, reduced crime, and were even able to gain intelligence from a mentee on active robbery suspects.

Our police department supports innovation in problem-solving; therefore, enforcement isn't the only metric in solving crime. It's imperative that we exercise procedural justice and work to restore the community on a continual basis. Our patrol officers attend crime-watch group meetings, present problem-solving outcomes at Compstat, and help crime victims heal. It's part of our policing culture."

Tarrick McGuire is currently an interim deputy chief of police with the Arlington, Texas Police Department (U.S.).

GETTING HELP WITH VIPER IDEAS

The five VIPER checklist components (victim support, intelligence gaps, prevention, enforcement, reassurance) are easy to grasp; however, populating these items is a little more challenging. But even though you are in command, you do not have to scavenge all of the ideas yourself. Collaborating with others to get inspiration does not rob you of the final decision authority, and there is value in casting your intellectual net a little wider, as the next two ideas suggest.

Developing hypotheses and the wisdom of crowds

Too often senior officers appear to dismiss the views of experienced cops simply because they are frontline foot soldiers and not apparently of sufficient rank to have ideas worthy of merit. To widen your intellectual net, incorporate patrol officers and others in your decision-making around crime problems (see Box 7.5). At the least, inclusion of your junior colleagues will increase the likelihood of their support when implementing your eventual plan.

BOX 7.5 UNDERSTANDING NORTHAMPTONSHIRE'S NIGHT-TIME ECONOMY VIOLENCE

"I became Northamptonshire Police's lead for violent crime reduction shortly after a new Police and Crime Commissioner introduced a 40% reduction target. Quite a challenge! We needed fresh eyes and so engaged an external academic to help address night-time town center violence. We brought in a number of officers from the front-line who were intimately familiar with the problems in the area. They helped me see the town centers in a different light. It was liberating to recognize what was really happening and not just make assumptions based on the things cops were called to. By looking at causes, I began to see some 'bad' venues as victims. The violence they experienced was often a result of staff trying to do the right thing. It wasn't just the result of customers fighting each other in poorly-run venues.

This insight led to a radical new approach working with clubs to manage drunks and supporting them to improve. I initially believed that my biggest challenges were to win the clubs' trust and help them learn without fearing prosecution. I also thought we had to convince officers to see themselves as a part of the night-time economy rather than an intervention when things went south. These were important but, in the end, I was wrong. The biggest challenge has been to sustain the changes without regressing to the old ways."

Dave Spencer is a chief inspector seconded to the College of Policing organizational development faculty. He was previously an operational chief inspector with Northamptonshire Police.

For a number of years, a hypothesis testing approach was promoted by the Jill Dando Institute for Crime Science. It has helped a number of police forces address challenging crime issues, such as Northamptonshire Police (see Box 7.5). It has subsequently been trialed by the Philadelphia Police Department (U.S.). A key component was the inclusion of officers with different experiences into the process. The stages Philadelphia employed are summarized in Box 7.6. As you can see, the officers were part of the front-end discussion of the problem, and sometimes tapped for ideas at the culmination of the process.

By including the opinions of a range of officers and stakeholders, the hypothesis testing approach, in a way, taps into the wisdom of crowds. Popularized by James Surowiecki's 2005 book of the same name,[12] the wisdom of crowds is the idea that the aggregated perspective of a diverse group can frequently perform better than any of the individuals in the group. Surowiecki demonstrates this with the tale of Sir Francis Galton's day out at a country fair in Plymouth, England in 1906. This is the same Francis Galton who first described regression to the mean as *regression to mediocrity*.

Galton stumbled upon a competition to guess the weight of an ox. He was given the nearly 800 submitted cards where entrants had

---

BOX 7.6 HYPOTHESIS TESTING STAGES

1   An *initial meeting* with numerous police participants from various ranks and experiences that generates 3–5 hypotheses. Frontline officers are essential.

2   A *recursive analytical phase* where an analyst explores each hypothesis in detail. This can involve interaction with experienced analysts at headquarters. Hypotheses are refined and tested until ready for reporting out.

3   A *reporting out meeting* to a subset of the original group to determine operational responses.

4   An *operational implementation phase* designed to supervise and drive the response implementation.[11]

written their guess. Even though in his mid-80s at this point in his life, Galton remained ever the scientist and aware of the possibility of flawed research data, writing:

> The judgments were unbiased by passion and uninfluenced by oratory and the like. The sixpenny fee deterred practical joking, and the hope of a prize and the joy of competition prompted each competitor to do his best. The competitors included butchers and farmers, some of whom were highly expert in judging the weight of cattle; others were probably guided by such information as they might pick up, and by their own fancies.[13]

The ox was slaughtered and dressed, weighing in at 1,198 pounds. When Galton calculated what he called the *middlemost* weight (what we now call the median value) where half the guesses were heavier and half were lighter, that value was 1,207 pounds. The middle of all 787 guesses was just nine pounds from the true weight.

Galton demonstrated that under the right circumstances, the combined efforts of a diverse group can outperform specific individuals, or at least do as well as the best of them.

Galton demonstrated that under the right circumstances, the combined efforts of a diverse group can outperform specific individuals, or at least do as well as the best of them. This collective intelligence allows poor estimates in one direction to be balanced by poor estimates in the other.

To tap into this resource, try pulling together four elements identified as necessary by Surowiecki. First, a *diversity of opinion* is essential so bringing together a range of stakeholders and people is important. This will help avoid groupthink. Second, the people in the process should have some *independence* so that their views are not simply mirroring others. Most cops defer to either rank or time served. As a result, you end up with little diversity. Give serious consideration to

BOX 7.7 REQUIREMENTS FOR A WISE CROWD

To bring together a diverse group that can help you tap into the wisdom of the crowd, ensure you have:

1   a diversity of opinion
2   independence of perspective
3   decentralization that brings different knowledge
4   an aggregation process.

having people submit ideas anonymously to ensure independence. It may remove the stifling effect your rank might inadvertently impose.

Decentralization is a fancy term for saying that people and systems you interact with should be able to act independently of the others. This means that participants in your process will bring a specialization and local knowledge not normally available from other stakeholders. Finally, you need a coordination process of *aggregation* to be able to bring all of this diversity and decentralized to a decision point (see Box 7.7).

Working with partnerships

The President's Task Force on 21st Century Policing noted that: "It will be through partnerships across sectors and at every level of government that we will find the effective and legitimate long-term solutions to ensuring public safety."[14] While working with partnerships is increasingly seen as essential for long-term crime reduction goals, many mid-level officers are initially unprepared for it. Much of the job prior to promotion involves solving issues single-handedly in the field.

On promotion, many officers feel like they have been thrust into a new world of 'slow-death-by-meeting.' Non-police groups tend to see the world differently, which can be jarring at first. But that doesn't necessarily mean they don't have valuable insights. Public health officials and community groups often spend considerable time on the street, and they can have useful input into potential strategies, especially around *victim support* and *reassurance* (V and R in VIPER).

Making a bland statement that you will 'work with partners' is not the same thing as clearly articulating what crime prevention mechanism they will influence.

Second, they may have resources that they can bring to bear on the problem. They may need cajoling or convincing to do so, but that is part of the soft skill set you will need to bring to the job of command. As former Philadelphia Police Commissioner Charles Ramsey was fond of saying: "I love it when I can get other government departments to spend their money to solve my problems." When identifying potential collaborators, a key question to ask yourself is, 'who brings what to the table?'

Not everyone invited to a meeting can necessarily add value. I suspect that there is an inverse relationship between the number of people on a committee and its effectiveness. You need to be explicit about what they can do. Making a bland statement that you will 'work with partners' is not the same thing as clearly articulating what crime prevention mechanism they will influence.

A third contribution of partnership working is the benefit of getting community and political support for your strategy. Community support for a new initiative might help offset friction later, especially with operations that have a strong enforcement component (see Box 4.5). Community partners can help spread a prevention message. It's not for nothing that the President's Task Force on 21st Century Policing recommended "law enforcement agencies should develop and adopt policies and strategies that reinforce the importance of community engagement in managing public safety."[14]

Police officers are inherently optimistic and hate only two things: how we do it right now, and change.

It's worth remembering that when you start trying new ideas that are innovative, some people with more traditional mindsets can feel a little discombobulated. Police officers are inherently optimistic and hate only two things: how we do it right now, and change. There is no shortage of traditionalists within the police service who have limited imagination and respect for new ideas. Police associations or unions may need to be consulted if you have operational strategies that involve significant changes to work practices or conventions.

This may all sound too challenging but remember that working with colleagues of different ranks and experience, or bringing in community partners, can enhance your knowledge and grow the range of VIPER options.

AN EXAMPLE MISSION AND VIPER RESPONSE

If you recall, Amy, our intrepid area commander, had a burglary problem in one of her housing projects. Box 7.8 shows an example mission statement and VIPER response. These are only example statements and responses and you should of course tailor yours to whatever problem you have.

BOX 7.8 AMY'S MISSION STATEMENT AND VIPER RESPONSES

In this example, mission statement items are identified with lower-case Roman numerals (i, ii, iii, and iv) and VIPER responses are shown with capital letters.

Operation Reducing Crime aims to make the community safer with (i) a 20% reduction in (ii) residential burglary at the Waramanga public housing project.

The Victim support (V) strategy of (iii) crime prevention officer visits to burgled homes will contribute by (iv) increasing the effort required by offenders to commit repeat victimization. By filling Intelligence gaps (I) with (iii) informant interviews, analysis, and traffic enforcement, we will (iv) increase our understanding of offender behavior and identify more burglars. Prevention (P) through (iii) gated alleys and parking areas will (iv) limit non-resident access to the targeted area. The Enforcement strategy (E) of (iii) plain-clothes patrols will contribute to the mission by (iv) heightening the risks for offenders by increasing the likelihood of arrest. In addition, (iii) uniform officer patrols will (iv) provide a visible deterrence to opportunist offenders. Finally, we will increase Reassurance (R) with (iii) community support officer visits and media liaison support (iv) assigned to reinforce the message that the police service is responding to the problem and taking an active role in reducing it.

Specific VIPER tasks are:

Victim support   A crime prevention officer to visit each burglary victim and offer situational crime prevention advice in order to reduce risk of repeat victimization. Victim support services agency to contact each victim. Responding officers to distribute business cards with victim support details.

Intelligence gaps   Officers with confidential informants living or active within one mile of the target area to ask their CIs about recent burglary activity. Crime analysis to check recent prison release data for known burglars with ties to the area. Traffic patrol tasked with vehicular enforcement in order to identify suspect vehicles in the area. Reporting officers to enhance crime reports with specific information on modus operandi and home access points.

Prevention   City council be asked to fund alley gates to prevent easy access to rear of vulnerable properties in the housing project. Discuss with neighborhood management possibility of installing access barriers to resident car parks. Crime prevention officer to call on houses adjoining victimized locations and offer prevention advice to reduce near repeat victimization risk.

Enforcement	Burglary units to patrol alleyways in plain clothes during daylight hours when most burglaries occur. Uniform patrol officers to conduct traffic enforcement on roads leading to and from housing project for at least one hour per shift. Burglary team to actively enforce existing warrants on known burglars within one mile of the housing project.
Reassurance	Community support officers to visit neighborhood watch meetings and describe police initiatives. Community officers to patrol neighborhood in afternoons when parents and school children are around. Media liaison to relate police response to local newspapers (excluding role of plain-clothes units).

CHAPTER SUMMARY

- Build a clear mission statement for your operation that explains outcomes and how they will be achieved. It should explicitly tie activities with the mechanism for how they will impact outcomes.
- Support for crime victims can improve cooperation with police and provide other positive benefits for law enforcement.
- Filling intelligence gaps can improve knowledge around crime problems and enhance the effectiveness of future decision-making.
- When thinking about prevention, ask yourself, "If you had no police or enforcement resources that you could deploy, how could you reduce the problem?"
- Enforcement is frequently a short-term, stop-gap measure that can become a significant resource drain.
- Working with colleagues of different ranks and experience, or bringing in community partners can enhance your knowledge and grow the range of VIPER options.

REFERENCES

1 Ratcliffe, J.H., *Intelligence-Led Policing* (2nd edition). 2016, Abingdon, Oxon.: Routledge.

2 Forrester, D., M. Chatterton, and K. Pease, *The Kirkholt Burglary Prevention Project, Rochdale.* 1988, Crime Prevention Unit (Home Office): London.

3 IACP, *Enhancing Law Enforcement Response to Victims: A 21st Century Strategy.* nd, International Association of Chiefs of Police: Washington, D.C.

4 Mayne, S.R., *Instructions to "The New Police of the Metropolis."* 1829, London: Metropolitan Police.

5 Rodgers, D., *Slum Wars of the 21st Century: Gangs, Mano Dura and the new urban geography of conflict in Central America.* Development and Change, 2009. **40**(5): p. 949–76.

6 Herrington, V. and A. Millie, *Applying Reassurance Policing: Is it "Business as Usual"?* Policing and Society, 2006. **16**(2): p. 146–63.

7 Innes, M., *Reinventing tradition? Reassurance, neighbourhood security and policing.* Criminal Justice, 2004. **4**(2): p. 151–71.

8 Innes, M., *What's your problem? Signal crimes and citizen-focused problem solving.* Criminology and Public Policy, 2005. **4**(2): p. 187–200.

9 Tuffin, R., J. Morris, and A. Poole, *An evaluation of the impact of the National Reassurance Policing Programme.* 2006, Research, Development and Statistics Directorate (Home Office): London.

10 Millie, A. and V. Herrington. *Reassurance Policing: Views from the shop floor,* in British Society of Criminology conference proceedings. 2004. Portsmouth, U.K.

11 Philadelphia Police Department, *Smart Policing Initiative: Final Report.* 2017, Bureau of Justice Assistance: Washington, D.C.

12 Surowiecki, J., *The Wisdom of Crowds.* 2005, New York: Anchor.

13 Galton, F., *Vox Populi.* Nature, 1907. **75**(1949): p. 450–51.

14 President's Task Force on 21st Century Policing, *Final Report of the President's Task Force on 21st Century Policing.* 2015, Office of Community Oriented Policing Services: Washington, D.C.

8

DEPLOYING A CRIME REDUCTION STRATEGY

By this point you should have completed the first three stages of PANDA. With the *Problem scan* stage, you identified the range of problems in your command and decided whether they were chronic, spikes, or panics. To make sure they were unique problems you examined them against the CHEERS checklist. With each significant problem, you analyzed them—the first A in PANDA—centered on your VOLTAGE analysis. From the analysis you formed a mission statement regarding the outcome you want to change, and you used the *Nominate strategy* part of PANDA to identify your VIPER responses. Great work so far.

It's now time for D-Day. This is where you *deploy* (the D in PANDA) your crime reduction strategy. Many crime reduction operations fail because too much is left to individual interpretation, is ambiguous, or there is a lack of clarity about who will do what. Vagueness kills projects. The leader's role is to balance the overall task while being clear about assignments and ensuring the role of each individual is clearly defined and understood. This chapter addresses the deployment phase by focusing on the acronym GOALS for five components of a good deployment.

Many crime reduction operations fail because too much is left to individual interpretation, is ambiguous, or there is a lack of clarity about who will do what.

IMPLEMENTING YOUR GOALS

The GOALS (Table 8.1) components stress accountability and specifics. The importance of assigning individual or key personnel to specific tasks is hard to overstate.

Ground commander (G)

You will note from Table 8.1 that a key part of the process is the naming of individual people to tasks. The ground commander (G in GOALS) is the single individual who everyone knows is in

Table 8.1 The GOALS checklist

Ground commander	Name the person who will be responsible for the deployment of your strategy. This might be you. You can assign different people to different VIPER tasks, but the important accountability and clarity stems from individual assignments.
Objectives	Your objectives should be related to your VIPER elements in your strategy. Nominate SMART objectives before deploying your solution. This will keep you more honest in the *Assess* stage of PANDA. SMART objectives are explained in the following section.
Analyst	Assign someone who will be responsible for tracking the data during the implementation, and the analysis on completion. They can also gather and collate feedback and intelligence.
Limits	Clearly state the spatial limit of the strategy, and select an achievable time frame so everyone understands when the strategy will be assessed and reviewed. You can also stress operational limits such as when to exercise discretion.
Support	Be clear about what support is needed, and who is responsible for the provision of that support.

charge of the project. You can either nominate someone else for the role, or take it on yourself. The key is to have one point of contact held accountable for the implementation of your VIPER strategies. If you can give them a role in designing parts of the strategy or how their task will be implemented, this will increase their 'buy-in' and commitment to the project (Box 8.3).

In large projects, this person could delegate individual responsibility for each VIPER element to others in the project, or you could assign command for various pieces of a large operation. Leadership shouldn't be anonymous, and it is important that a named individual is known to all as the command person on the ground for your operation. When anonymity reduces individual effort for intellectual tasks, it is called 'cognitive loafing.'[1] In a nutshell, if people expect to have to justify their views or have their work assessed, they increase their cognitive effort. They might do it to seek more praise and recognition, or alternatively to avoid embarrassment and the subsequent damage to their self-esteem.[2] Either way, increasing personal responsibility seems to encourage people to up their effort, as recalled by Arif Nawaz (see Box 8.1).

BOX 8.1 A HAND-PICKED TEAM PRODUCES RESULTS

"I took over an area with 80,000 university students and was told to keep them safe. They are the city's largest victim group for domestic burglaries and street robberies, yet I went in without an instruction manual or real understanding of the issues. I was immersed into a complex multi-agency world and told to chair the monthly meetings. Initially, it felt as though I, and policing, were being held to account for things for which I had no knowledge.

I had to learn a new partnership language and quickly develop relationships with key partners outside of the meetings. I brought together police and partner analysts along with experienced officers. Their analysis provided nuanced details such as how differing ethnic groups were susceptible to different crime types as a result of cultural

behaviors. It was clear our traditional approach of focusing crime prevention advice on potential victims was next to useless.

Instead, I selected a bespoke offender targeting team led by a
hand-picked inspector and two sergeants supported by a dedicated
analyst. They created an effective and vibrant team that delivered
results on the ground. The quality and enthusiasm of the team's leaders was critical to its success as was their belief in my vision and our
shared values."

*Arif Nawaz is currently a chief superintendent with Greater
Manchester Police (U.K.), and the branch head of organizational learning and workforce development.*

Objectives (O)

Your objectives should be both SMART and outcome focused. There
are numerous variations of SMART objectives. In this book I'm referring to objectives that are *Specific, Measurable, Achievable, Realistic,* and
Time-bound (Box 8.2). Let's look at an example. A superintendent in
Australia (where random breath tests are legal) could give a patrol
sergeant this instruction: "We have an increase in traffic accidents,
so set up a couple of roadblocks and do some breath tests." At least
the overarching reason for the work is given; however, the remain-
ing instructions are too vague. Where should the breath tests be, and
when should they be completed?

A better (SMART) instruction would be: "To try and reduce the
number of nighttime traffic accidents involving alcohol, by the end of
this month set up at least five, two-hour long breath-test roadblocks
on Northbourne Avenue, starting between 10 pm and midnight. Make
sure that we explain to each driver why we are doing the stops."

BOX 8.2 SMART OBJECTIVES

Specific
Measurable
Achievable
Realistic
Time-bound

This SMART objective (see Box 8.2) not only allows the superintendent to hold the sergeant accountable to a specific goal, but it is also a clearer operational plan that can be reported to executive management or the community if necessary. Other aspects of the SMART acronym are important, such as the setting of realistic goals.

By focusing on outcomes rather than outputs, you will also avoid the trap of offering perverse incentives that can skew your crime reduction effort. Harmful negative outputs occur frequently, such as when commanders try and drive productivity by setting targets for traffic tickets, pedestrian investigations, or arrests. Demands for quotas can infuriate the public and police officers alike. As former Baltimore officer-turned-academic Pete Moskos has written, quotas "insult police professionalism and contribute to community hatred of the police. In a quota-driven system, police tend to see all citizens, even the good ones, as potential stats."[3] Compstat, and related meetings, can easily skew good intentions into bad decisions. It's always worth remembering why you joined the job: good outcomes for the community.

Analyst (A)

As with the ground commander, you should select a person to take on the role of *analyst* (the A in GOALS). They should monitor the ongoing tracking of data that can help you ensure your project is being implemented as planned. This same data can also be used to assess the project success at a later date. There is no need for them to be a crime analyst *per se*. They could be a sworn officer who you assign to the role of data and intelligence collection for the duration of the project, as Pedro Guillén did in Box 8.3.

When the Philadelphia Police Department asked me to assess the impact of an acoustic gunshot detection system, they assigned a single analyst to collect the data throughout the pilot phase. Matt's attention to detail and task focus was marvelous and it helped to have a single point of contact for both technical questions and data consistency. Knowing Matt, he would have done a sterling job even if he had been part of a team assigned to collect project data. But sometimes that doesn't happen with shared responsibility or where there is no individual accountability. When people have a shared accountability and where their specific contribution will not be assessed, they tend to put in less effort. This can be for both physical tasks as well as intellectual tasks. Like cognitive loafing for individuals, social psychologists even have a term for it: 'social loafing.' This has been demonstrated from business decision-making[4] to (of all things) shouting.[5]

This is why assigning an analyst is so important. If you rely on the normal procedures within your police department for your project data collection, you may be losing the opportunity to have a focused pair of eyes on your strategy. This is the same idea as the thinking behind making sure you have a ground commander in charge of the implementation 'on the ground' (the G in GOALS).

Limits (L)

Limits are important to avoid mission creep (when a task or operation gradually grows beyond the bounds of the original goals). For example, if designing a saturation foot patrol in a bar and entertainment area, some of the components you could state include:

1 The spatial limits of the foot patrol area and when officers can go beyond these boundaries.
2 The temporal limits in terms of the days and times of the patrol.

3   The chronological limits in terms of when the overall operation will conclude.

4   Procedural limits that define the activities you want, the nature of your enforcement plan, and how and when discretion should be exercised.

5   Any other policies and limits relevant to your strategy.

Without clear guidance on the where and when, officers will revert back to their varied opinions or experience, which gets us away from your data analysis and the tenets of evidence-based policing (see Chapter 10). And cops have a tendency to wander a bit, especially on foot patrol, as we discovered in Philadelphia.[6] You might want to give officers some latitude if you have evidence of problems displacing to neighboring streets, but you can include limits on this in your operational strategy.

Procedural limits might also be relevant to your operation. You might want to provide direction to officers so that they engage in procedurally-just proactive work that demonstrates a sense of perspective (for a discussion of procedural justice, see Chapter 11). Let's say you are setting enforcement goals in a nighttime entertainment area. You could set limits on what infractions should be enforced and when you are willing to allow officers to use their discretion. Directives like this can maintain a sense of perspective that can prevent over-zealous policing that can undermine police legitimacy.

Eighty percent of police agencies partner with non-profit or non-government organizations.

Support (S)

Finally, you should include in your operational plan some indication of additional support you need or expect. This will make it clear to other departments or groups where their contribution is expected to be. Eighty percent of police agencies partner with non-profit or non-government organizations,[7] but you cannot expect their understanding of your expectations to be as clear as you might expect from police colleagues. If you have promises of support, get the specifics of their contribution and their agreement in writing, even if only in email. It will make your expectations of them clear, which is important in preventing miscommunication.

Writing down exactly what, where, when, and why you are including them will help spell out their role and prevent ambiguity and confusion. It has other benefits. If you are successful at reducing crime, other commanders will want to know what you did. This will help as a memory jog. It will also help you evaluate your own project (as explained in Chapters 9 and 10).

BOX 8.3 DELEGATE AND ASSIGN TO GET THE BEST FROM PEOPLE

"I was made the chief of a tactical unit with the mission to apprehend gang members in Zacatecoluca (El Salvador). In the National Civil Police (PNC), commanders tend not to delegate—they just give general orders. So, I wanted to work in a different way. I designated one particular agent to do the intelligence tasks, and another to communicate with our rural population. That agent can easily talk to people, and he could convince folk to be associated with the police, and to become partners with us. I specifically assigned another to manage the formal documents because that was their skill area.

We are told to issue commands, but it is not the same as delegating individually. Generally announcing orders doesn't work. You have to choose the right person, and convince that agent of the importance of the job they are going to do. Then they own it, even if it is hard or difficult. The agent will work diligently even though it might be outside business hours. You choose him or her and they feel empowered, proud about the task, and committed.

Together we are doing the job of removing the priority targets from the community. It's an ongoing challenge, and we can't remove all of the gang members, but we can get the key people."

Pedro Antonio Guillén Meléndez is a sub-inspector in El Salvador's National Civil Police (PNC) and the head of a tactical unit in La Paz delegation.

ONCE THE STRATEGY IS UNDERWAY

Once your strategy is underway, the hard work hasn't finished. It might be just beginning. As a supervisor (and especially if you are the ground commander for the strategy) there are a number of factors to consider, each of which will have a substantial impact on the outcome of the operation.

Supervision style in the field

The quality and direction of immediate field supervision (especially from sergeants) may be a vital factor in the successful implementation of any crime reduction strategy. Engel's observations of patrol supervisors revealed four general approaches.[8] *Traditional supervisors* are focused on controlling their officers, expect productivity and paperwork, and are predominantly task-focused (see Chapter 11). They prefer to give instructions and take command of situations in the field. *Innovative supervisors* are more interested in community activity and focused on mentoring and developing their officers, especially around problem-solving. As Engel notes, they "have more perceived power in the organization and have positive views of subordinates." *Supportive supervisors* tend to shield their officers from what they perceive as poor management. They score highly on motivation, creativity, and promoting teamwork. They are more focused on the team and individual than the task.

Active supervisors haven't really made the move to supervisor, and still engage with patrol action and street work. They tend to take command of situations they roll up on, and believe that they have power in the organization. They tend to have less inspirational motivation. A potential problem with active supervisors is that, while influential, they may not necessarily be a positive influence on your project. Engel found that when an active supervisor was present, officers were significantly more likely to use force against a suspect.

It may be useful to consider the style you want to adopt or encourage in other supervisors. If you are of sufficient rank that you can select supervisors to manage your projects for you, consider their style against what outcomes you want. If you cannot select supervisors or officers, your feedback could encourage them to take on or mimic some of the characteristics your project needs. In a recent study of hot spots policing in London train stations, greater compliance and patrol efficiency was achieved at one station when a supervisor gave officers feedback on how often they were in the target areas. The successful station "had experienced strong and consistent leadership for several years with the same inspector responsible for the location for a prolonged period. This leader was well respected for his knowledge and experience."[9] The right people matter.

Demonstrate investment in the plan

During one policing experiment, my colleagues and I found a number of officers questioning how much their leadership cared about the project. One officer said, "I just don't see investment from the police department on this. It doesn't seem like they are taking it seriously." If you have devoted energy to putting together your VIPER responses, you can undermine that effort if you don't recruit others to the strategy or buy into your own plan. Here are some ideas.

Visit frequently

One way to demonstrate your investment in the plan is to visit the crime hot spot frequently (if you are addressing a crime hot spot problem). It shows enthusiasm for the plan and builds credibility. It may also allow you to gain insights that can help the learning process. It's an opportunity to see how enthusiastically the troops are implementing your strategy. In other types of operation, being seen at project meetings and visiting with non-police partners demonstrates commitment and, again, can provide insights into commitment from your partnership agencies. At the least, your presence will reinforce accountability, which can combat social loafing.

Avoid mission creep

Good crime prevention can take time, so while your well-considered operation is still underway, it is likely that other pressures and crime spikes are taking place. There is a tendency for mission creep to bleed into the original operation. You may find yourself under pressure to expand target areas or change the operational plan you designed using VIPER and GOALS. This is frequently a mistake, because it dilutes the impact of the original plan, and without a strong analytical phase it is often a weak solution for the emerging crime problem. Try and resist mission creep unless the implications have been thoroughly evaluated.

Stick to a definite review timetable

After a while in policing, I started to notice that the solution to most crime problems was to form a squad. Whenever we had an emerging problem, a squad would be formed to tackle the new threat, like a motor vehicle crime squad, a gang unit, or a repeat offender team.

Squads are easy to form, but in the absence of robust evaluation they are the devil to disband. Without an evaluation and evidence that the crime problem has dissipated, the tendency is for leadership to believe that the squad hasn't had enough time to work, rather than the equally likely possibility that they aren't effective against the problem. Like a squad, your new strategy can easily become a drain on resource and effort. To avoid this, you should establish and stick to a definite timetable that includes an evaluation. Without evaluating the effectiveness of your strategy, you are never going to know if you are being successful. You will end up with a squad that exists, but whose worth is unknown. We look at evaluating strategies in the next chapter.

Squads are easy to form, but in the absence of robust evaluation they are the devil to disband. . . . To avoid this, you should establish and stick to a definite timetable that includes an evaluation.

CHAPTER SUMMARY

- Assign a ground commander with overall responsibility for the strategy implementation. You can assign different people to take on various aspects of your VIPER strategy in larger projects.
- Objectives should be both SMART and outcome focused. SMART objectives are specific, measurable, achievable, realistic, and time-bound.
- Be explicit about the support you need or are getting from outside agencies. Get their commitments in writing if possible.
- Be cognizant of various leadership styles in the field and try to adopt an appropriate style.
- Visit the site or relevant meetings frequently.
- Avoid mission creep.
- Stick to a definite review timetable so you can see if your strategy is working.

REFERENCES

1 Weldon, E. and G.G. Gargano, *Cognitive effort in additive task groups: The effects of shared responsibility on the quality of multiattribute judgments.* Organizational Behavior and Human Decision Processes, 1985. **36**(3): p. 348–61.

2 Tetlock, P.E., *Accountability and complexity of thought.* Journal of Personality and Social Psychology, 1983. **45**(1): p. 74–83.

3 Moskos, P., *Cop in the Hood: My Year Policing Baltimore's Eastern District.* 2008, Princeton, NJ: Princeton University Press.

4 Price, K.H., *Decision responsibility, task responsibility, identifiability, and social loafing.* Organizational Behavior & Human Decision Processes, 1987. **40**(3): p. 330–46.

5 Williams, K., S.G. Harkins, and B. Latané, *Identifiability as a deterrant to social loafing: Two cheering experiments.* Journal of Personality and Social Psychology, 1981. **40**(2): p. 303–11.

6 Sorg, E.T., et al., *Explaining dosage diffusion during hot spot patrols: An application of optimal foraging theory to police officer behavior.* Justice Quarterly, 2017. **34**(6): p. 1044–68.

7 Police Executive Research Forum, *Future Trends in Policing.* 2014, Office of Community Oriented Policing Services: Washington, D.C.

8 Engel, R.S., *The effects of supervisory styles on patrol officer behavior.* Police Quarterly, 2000. **3**(3): p. 262–93.

9 de Brito, C. and B. Ariel, *Does tracking and feedback boost patrol time in hot spots? Two tests.* Cambridge Journal of Evidence-Based Policing, 2017. **1**(4): p. 244–62.

9

ASSESSING YOUR OUTCOMES

THE OILRIG CHECKLIST

Don't panic. Everyone recoils from evaluations. If they are personnel evaluations, we want to get them over and done with. If they are operational, we tend to avoid them entirely. Assessments of police operations contain the potential for a lot of risk with scant reward. On the downside, you might find that you weren't successful, or in the case of some strategies (like Scared Straight*) made things worse. In extreme cases, not being successful might be temporarily career limiting. On the positive side, however, you might actually discover whether you were successful in abating the crime problem. Some officers have found sharing this knowledge with colleagues to be career-enhancing. Demonstrating some crime reduction benefits might even improve morale (yours and others). After all, isn't that why you joined the job?

The second 'A' in PANDA is *Assess outcomes*. The OILRIG checklist in this chapter is the backbone of your assessment, but is designed to do more than help you discover whether you achieved your original mission; it will help you make better decisions the next time. You might not have been as successful as you hoped, but the key to ben-efiting from failure is to learn from the experience. While the 'O' examines if you achieved your outcomes, the other components are included so you can review what worked, what didn't, and how you might improve your crime reduction strategy should you need to give it another go. The OILRIG checklist is shown in Box 9.1 along with some example questions to consider for each stage. You can no doubt think of others.

BOX 9.1 OILRIG CHECKLIST FOR ASSESSING CRIME REDUCTION EFFECTS

Component	Considerations
Outcomes achieved?	Did you achieve your stated outcomes? Refer back to your mission statement to remember what you set out to achieve.
Implemented as planned?	Whether you were successful or not, were your strategy objectives implemented as planned? Did you get the support from partners you expected?
Lessons learned?	Are there any lessons to be learned regarding choice of objective, implementation strategy, or perhaps sustainability of your success moving forward?
Results acceptable?	Whether or not your objectives were successful, are the overall outcome results acceptable? Even partial success may achieve good outcomes and allow you to prioritize resources elsewhere.
Intelligence gained?	Refer to the 'I' in VIPER. Did you gain intelligence that might improve a future deployment?
GOALS to be revised?	Should your GOALS be revised or revisited? Different personnel? Adjust support? Deploy for a longer period of time?

Outcomes achieved? (O)

Hopefully, back when you were selecting your GOALS in Chapter 8, your objectives were focused on an outcome. Not only are your outcomes the focus of your objectives in GOALS, they also feature in the O in OILRIG—the checklist we use in this chapter to assess what has been gained in your crime reduction efforts.

In formal terms you should conduct an outcome evaluation (sometimes called an impact evaluation). An outcome evaluation tells you if you moved the needle in terms of your crime or disorder outcomes. The evaluation might also reveal if there were any unintended consequences, both positive or negative. If you selected outcome-focused SMART objectives (specific, measurable, achievable, realistic, time-bound), and you have data that measures your outcome before and after your initiative began, then you are in a position to estimate if you were successful. The key here is the measurable component. You don't need an advanced degree in statistics, and you don't need to hire a statistical consultant. Let's look at an example.

> An outcome evaluation tells you if you moved the needle in terms of your crime or disorder outcomes.

Since she took over the district, our area commander Amy recognized not only a burglary problem but also a worrying trend in violence (the first few points in Figure 9.1). Before she could initiate a PANDA process, she was pressured into a saturation patrol and enforcement strategy by her executives at a Compstat meeting. She started it in May, as shown by the arrow in Figure 9.1. Some time later the chief wants to know if all the extra overtime (input) and arrests (output) resulted in a violence reduction (outcome).

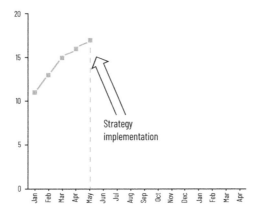

Figure 9.1 Monthly crime counts in one housing project (A)

You might think Amy can simply compare how many crimes occurred in the months prior to her effort, and the months since the operation has been running. This is quite common, but it is also inadequate. This before-and-after measure doesn't account for the seasonality of crime. For example, in general, it's known that violence tends to increase in summer months. Amy plots the violence in the housing project (A) for the two years since her enforced operation and can see this seasonal fluctuation (Figure 9.2). There is also a general downward trend. She could measure each subsequent May (the dotted vertical lines) and report that crime is down. But unfortunately, Amy doesn't know if this was due to the operation. Let me explain why.

We know that some crime types can exhibit seasonality. They can also have an upward or downward trend (like the long-term downward trend in crime over decades that you saw in the first chapter in Figure 1.1). Crime is rarely random, but aggregate crime counts over time can have a partially haphazard aspect to them—what researchers call *variance*. Because crime counts can be constantly shifting due to these factors of trend, seasonality, and variance,

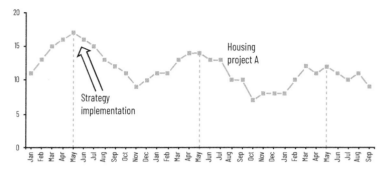

Figure 9.2 Extended monthly crime counts in one housing project (A)

simply comparing before an operation with afterwards is not an effective test. Amy needs to see what would have happened if she had done nothing at all, or more accurately, if things had been left to carry on as normal. She obviously can't do that in housing project A because that's where her operation is running. But she isn't running any significant operation in a similar housing project (B) half a mile away.

> *Because crime can be constantly shifting due to trend, seasonality,*
> *and variance, simply comparing before an operation with after-*
> *wards isn't an effective test.*

Because Amy wants to establish that housing project B is (what researchers call) a 'good match,' she confirms housing project (B) has about the same number of residents, that their demographics are roughly the same, and that there are no unusual activities or police operations running there, even though they are still patrolling and responding to calls. It's a good example of 'business-as-usual' and it will indicate what researchers call the *counterfactual*. This term

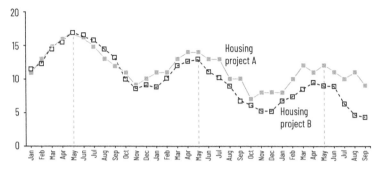

Figure 9.3 Monthly crime counts in two housing projects (A and B)

(sometimes also called the control) means that any changes in the crime patterns of housing project B can indicate what would have happened in housing project A, had Amy not run her operation and it had been policed as usual.

Unfortunately, you can see from Figure 9.3 that housing project A did not do as well over time as housing project B. In the long term, both housing projects appear to be getting generally safer. This could be due to economic changes in the region or better management of the locations. But because she was pressured to rush into a strategy without having a chance to do a thorough, thoughtful, and careful analysis, the enforcement strategy wasn't successful. Project A appeared to keep on par with project B initially, but over time the strategy seems to have made things a little worse. Perhaps the quality of the patrols dropped off over time as officers got bored with being in the same place for months, or perhaps the residents didn't take on responsibility for helping to reduce violence because they relied too heavily on the police.

Amy thinks that the patrols may have at least improved public confidence and trust in the police, and her anecdotal conversations with residents suggest this might be the case. Unfortunately, because of the rush to implement the strategy, this potentially positive outcome can't be confirmed because confidence in the police in the two housing projects wasn't measured before and after the operation. She makes a mental note to include public surveys, both before and after any future operations.

This 'evaluation' stuff may sound like a lot of work, but it's not too difficult. And it's important that we move beyond just 'rudimentary' measures of success (see Box 9.2). Other types of intervention may require different measures. But if you are doing an operation in a specific area (like a housing project or neighborhood) then you generally only need to measure crime before and after, in both the activity area and a control area (which will be your counterfactual). You can also measure the surrounding (buffer) area to check if there has been any displacement. The ABC spreadsheet described later in this chapter describes an easy way to measure your impact and any potential displacement or diffusion of benefits (these terms were described in Chapter 5).

BOX 9.2 TAPPING THE POWER OF DATA AND INFORMATION

"There is an unfortunate irony commonly found in modern policing. Police agencies often drop terms such as 'accountability' or 'transparency' but frequently fail to prepare supervisors and commanders to be truly accountable. Most agencies nowadays have an abundant supply of data. We have crime reports, calls for service, and some even have GPS data from patrol vehicle locations. The all-too-common shortfall, however, is failing to act on such data.

We frequently fall prey to executing crime reduction projects or other similar efforts without thorough follow-up once the project is complete. To be fair, rudimentary outcomes are sometimes measured, such as 'crime dropped 15% in the target area.' Results can be more robust for formal projects, but on the whole, even though we credit ourselves as being assertive problem-solvers, in policing there is rarely any assessment of operations. An attitude of 'moving onto the next thing' or, even worse, a return to the status quo, ultimately prevails. We put in all this effort yet never actually know whether we have really succeeded. Police departments often stress the power of data and information, but we seldom use it to properly evaluate or show the good work that our officers do."

Jonas Baughman is a sergeant with the Kansas City, Missouri Police Department (U.S.) assigned to the Office of the Chief of Police.

Implemented as planned? (I)

A key question should be "was your strategy implemented as you planned it?" In other words, did everyone do what they were supposed to? You might think this a bit redundant but it's important, especially if your strategy wasn't as successful as you hoped. While the O in OILRIG examines whether you got the outcomes you wanted (see the right side of Figure 9.4), the first I of OILRIG examines whether your inputs did as they were supposed to (the left side of Figure 9.4). Did your inputs generate the sort of outputs

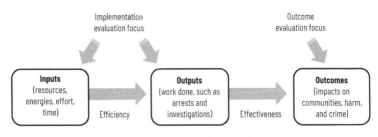

Figure 9.4 Implementation and outcome evaluation focus

(the middle box in the figure) that you thought would impact on the crime problem? You should do what is often called an implementation evaluation, also known as a process evaluation. This determines whether program activities have been implemented as intended and if you got the outputs you expected.

Because of the range of possible operations that readers of this book are likely to undertake, there isn't the space to run through every scenario, but there is a basic structure:

1 Review how the strategy was supposed to be implemented.
2 Identify whether the strategy was actually implemented as planned.
3 Determine how the strategy is currently operated.
4 Use the answers to these questions to determine your next steps.

Here are some questions that you might want to consider:

• What aspects of your original strategy were implemented as planned and what had to be changed?
• Why were any changes made?
• Did the strategy reach the right people (offenders or victims) or the right places (hot spots)?
• Did external partners do as they were asked to do?
• What was the level of enthusiasm of the participants?

This last question is important and will require you to look less at data, and spend more time talking to people. The quality of policing is as important as the quantity. Officers who engage with the community in a hot spot are worth much more to you than officers who park in a hiding spot and catch up on Twitter. Sometimes implementation mishaps can be well-meaning, as evident from Andy Parkes' tale in Box 9.3. Once you know whether your outcomes were achieved (O) and your strategy was implemented as planned (I), you can progress to reviewing the lessons learned.

BOX 9.3 IMPLEMENTATION FAILURES CAN BE WELL-MEANING

"My first local area command was a mixed blessing. The pride of being entrusted to look after 14,000 households, the challenge of having to deal with a burglary hot spot, and being held to account for it every week at crime meetings. I started with some evidence based analysis. I proved that, contrary to the expectation of many 'experts' (i.e. colleagues), many offences were at repeat or near repeat locations with similar MO: access from the rear using alleyways.

While I worked on the long-term goal of getting alley gates fitted, I also had a short-term plan for every burglary. The targeted house would get a 'Gold' service (window locks, window alarms, property marking etc.), adjacent houses a 'Silver' service (slightly less Gucci items), and those in the general vicinity a 'Bronze' response—leaflets with information about likely pattern of offending.

After a week, one of my well-meaning sergeants proudly announced that he had used up all of the (expensive) locks and alarms by giving everyone in the general vicinity the 'Gold' service. How could I shout at him? He was trying to help his community by doing what he thought was best. The lesson? Make sure you explain your expectations very clearly.

By the way, the alley gates worked."

Andy Parkes is a chief inspector with Leicestershire Police (U.K.) currently assigned to frontline response policing.

Lessons learned? (L)

If you were successful in achieving your outcome, everyone is going to want to know what you did, and how they can do it. If you were

Table 9.1 Lessons from process and outcome evaluations

		Objective achieved? (outcome evaluation result)	
		Yes	No
Implemented as planned? (process evaluation result)	Yes	The strategy worked. Spread the word!	Explore why the strategy didn't work.
	No	Either you got lucky (check the counterfactual) or the modified strategy has positive components.	Not a helpful result. You don't know if the strategy was poor, or if it would have worked if implemented properly.

not successful, you should figure out why. In either case, the implementation (or process) evaluation is important.

Table 9.1 shows that when you get a bad outcome *and* your project was not implemented as you planned it, it's difficult to draw any firm conclusions. You really don't know whether you designed an unsuccessful strategy, or if it would have worked had it been implemented properly. If that is the case, check back with the implementation evaluation and ask if it would ever have been implemented properly. Sometimes, we are a bit too optimistic about what is possible and what our organization—and other groups—are capable of supporting. A post-mortem with colleagues and agency partners is a good way to identify useful lessons (see Box 9.4).

Results acceptable? (R)

In this section of OILRIG, you should review everything you have learned. This combines the outcome evaluation, any additional crime or disorder outcomes observed, the reliability of your data and intelligence, the accuracy of your VOLTAGE analysis, any displacement or diffusion of benefits, the contributions of outside police departments or other government agencies, the enthusiasm of the participants, and the sustainability of the program into the long run. In other

BOX 9.4 CONDUCTING A POST-MORTEM

One way to learn lessons from an operation is to conduct a post-mortem. If you can do this impartially and without assigning blame, it can be a great tool to assess what worked and what didn't, how your strategy was implemented, and how you can move forward. Boon's[1] tips for a useful post-mortem include:

- Choose a suitable venue that limits distractions and in which people can be comfortable.
- Plan debriefing sessions that take into account the original objectives and the extent to which they were achieved.
- Invite a broad range of participants and not just people who were involved in the design of the strategy.
- If you think your rank might intimidate participants, delegate the role of moderator to someone more suitable.
- Set time limits and be realistic about what you can achieve in the time allocated.
- Use data to support any conclusions about the operation, and then note positive and negative reactions from participants.
- Exercise interpersonal skills to encourage feedback in a positive and non-threatening manner.
- Do not dismiss any feedback out of hand, even if it is unfair or biased.

A few questions that you might consider include:

- Were there any unintended outcomes?
- If you were to repeat the strategy, what would you do differently?
- Were there any barriers to implementation that you did not anticipate?
- Was the time frame appropriate?

words, review the totality of the project and determine answers to the following questions:

- Would you recommend this strategy to your colleagues?

- Are there circumstances where you think this strategy should not be used?
- Under what context (conditions) would it work best?
- Did you satisfactorily resolve the crime problem?

If the answer to the last question is 'yes' then congratulations! If the answer is 'no', then the last two parts of the OILRIG checklist become particularly important.

Intelligence gained? (I)

If you were not successful in achieving your strategy's goals, then at least gaining some useful intelligence on the problem can be a silver lining. A key aspect of intelligence is context. Intelligence starts as information that, when analyzed, has value because of the context in which you use it. In other words, an offender-focused strategy that takes down a violent drug gang might fail to quell the violence. But learning from confidential informants that when the drug corners became vacant other gangs fought to take over the territory is useful. You learn that just clearing corners may not be successful and that a more holistic strategy is needed.

If you did not gain any useful intelligence, it is worth conducting a post-mortem on why. There could be a number of reasons for this, and you should determine why you haven't been able to learn from the strategy. To Box 9.4 you could add questions related to the intelligence gathering:

- Were the P and A in PANDA reflected in what was seen on the ground?
- Did you assign resources to the I part of your VIPER strategy?
- Were the resources you assigned suitable for the task?
- Did you assign suitable resources, but they didn't do as they were asked?
- Was there a mechanism for them to feedback what they learned?
- Was there someone who could make sense of the feedback?

Gathering useful intelligence from an ongoing operation is not a task, it is a process. Take time to understand the process, so that you can improve on filling your intelligence gaps in the future.

GOALS to be revised? (G)

A reminder that your GOALS were; *Ground commander*, *Objectives*, *Analyst*, *Limits*, and *Support*. Table 9.2 lists each of these alongside a number of example questions you might want to ask of your GOALS.

The importance of reviewing your GOALS is to prevent repeating the same mistakes. While the intelligence gained (I) question is about improving knowledge about the criminal environment, this section of OILRIG is about learning how to improve the entire process. This is your opportunity to develop how you and your agency addresses crime reduction problems. Be warned that your findings from this part of the OILRIG process can sometimes reveal you might have been too optimistic in your expectations of outside agencies . . . or

Table 9.2 Questions to ask of your GOALS

Ground commander	Did your ground commander display an appropriate leadership style (see page 157)? Were they knowledgeable about the strategy? Did they buy into the strategy and lead it enthusiastically?
Objectives	Were your objectives outcome focused? Were they SMART? Did you decide the objectives using a transactional or transformational leadership style (see Chapter 11)?
Analyst	Was a suitable person assigned? Was data capture a priority for them? Did they have the skills to give you the answers you needed?
Limits	Were the spatial and temporal limits appropriate? Did you have a mechanism to learn if they were not?
Support	Was any support requested by you provided? Did the support provided function as expected? Did external partners perform as requested?

colleagues. Remember the words of famed NYPD detective Jack Maple: "The story is the same in any police department: Forty percent of the force hide behind their desks. Another 40 percent perform competently but without passion and without having much impact. Ten percent hate the job so much that they try to destroy everything positive that somebody else might try to accomplish. The final 10 percent treat the job like a vocation: and those 10 percent do 90 percent of the work."[2]

LEARNING FROM FAILURE

If you are tackling a chronic problem, chances are that your predecessors have had a go at it long before you got to your area. You might join them in not being as successful as you hoped with your first attempt at fixing the problem. Don't be disheartened! In his book *Black Box Thinking*, Matthew Syed has a marvelous story about James Dyson, the successful engineer and inventor of efficient vacuum cleaners that have made him a billionaire.[3] Dyson's dual-zone vacuum cleaner started as the result of first recognizing the failure of the existing process (in his case for vacuuming his house). Even while smart and inspired with a goal, it took years and hundreds of experiments with different sizes and shapes of vacuum to come up with the perfect solution. As Syed notes, Dyson built 5,127 prototype versions before his cyclone technology was ready to deploy into a marketable vacuum cleaner.

There are a couple of key lessons from Dyson's example. First, innovation is often driven when we identify a failure in an existing system. It might start with you asking: "Why do we always do it like that?" or "There must be a better way to do this." Second, while Dyson had a couple of revolutionary insights, his achievement was largely one of tenacity and incremental improvement. You could argue that he 'failed' 5,126 times, but importantly he learned a lesson each time. He built his knowledge and ideas with each prototype, tweaking and developing new insights with each iteration.

This is why the development of intelligence gaps is a vital part of the VIPER checklist. It is designed to help you improve your understanding so that even if you fail to reduce crime this time, you will be armed with more information next time around. It is why 'lessons learned' and 'intelligence gained' are parts of the OILRIG checklist.

Where next?

There are a number of possible directions at this point. When you asked yourself if you successfully resolved the crime problem in the 'R' part of OILRIG (Results acceptable?) and answered in the affirmative, then congratulations! See about contributing to the profession in the last chapter of this book and tell the rest of us about your success. You should also return to the P component of PANDA and do a new problem scan of the criminal environment. Don't assume that the scan you originally completed is still relevant. Crime is dynamic and the situation may have changed.

If you were not successful, then take a deep breath or two. Don't fret – you are not the first commander to have less success than anticipated. It may have come as a bit of a shock, but you gave it a go and have earned a moment to pick yourself up and dust yourself off.

When ready, take time to consider where the process might not have worked. The OILRIG checklist is designed to help you figure this out, and discussing this with colleagues and friends in partner agencies can give you a broader perspective. If your initial analysis had some flaws and you have since gained some intelligence through your operation, return to the first A in PANDA and conduct a new and revised analysis of the problem.

You might want to choose different strategies. If so, review VIPER at the nominate stage (N) of PANDA. If you believe your analysis and VIPER strategy were sound, but you had an implementation problem, then return to the D in PANDA and revise your deployment. This approach can be effective if you have an analyst who can keep you updated with current progress as your strategy is unfolding. These avenues are shown as black arrows in Figure 9.5.

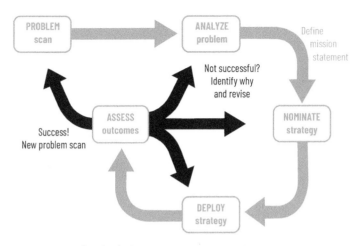

Figure 9.5 Optional paths from assessing outcomes stage

THE ABC SPREADSHEET

To help you conduct a simple evaluation, the website for this book has a spreadsheet designed in Microsoft Excel that is free to download. To use the spreadsheet and estimate how effective your initiative has been, you only need to figure out six numbers. The ABC spreadsheet requires before and after counts of crime or disorder in Activity, Buffer, and Control areas (hence ABC).

Figure 9.6 shows one example of how you might construct these areas. Some years ago I worked with FBI gang task force officers to evaluate the impact of Operation Thumbs Down, a take-down of the Rollin' 30's Harlem Crips gang in South Central Los Angeles.[4] The activity area (the gang territory) is shown in blue. Gang task force officers were worried that if they concentrated in this activity area, crime might be displaced to surrounding streets. The research evidence is clear that displacement is unlikely (see Chapter 5); even so, we estimated a buffer area that the local LAPD officers thought the most likely place crime might move to (with the blue border).

The third area is a control area. This is the counterfactual that I mentioned earlier. Crime changes here represent what would have

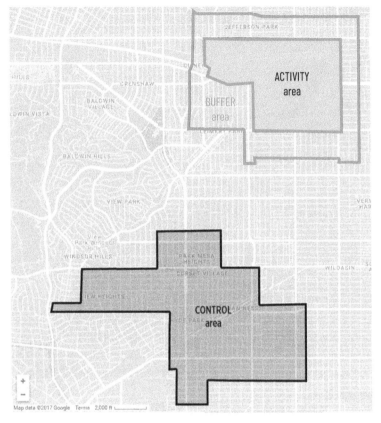

Figure 9.6 Example activity, buffer, and control areas

happened in the activity area if the task force had not been in operation. These are the normal fluctuations in crime under a 'business
as usual' scenario. This doesn't mean policing wasn't occurring—it
just represents the usual day-to-day level of enforcement. You should
gather and monitor the same data for each area.

Some thought has to go into the control area. Comparing an urban
bar district to a suburban gated community isn't realistic. For Operation Thumbs Down we selected a comparable gang area controlled
by the Rollin' 60's street gang. It was in South Central Los Angeles,

Table 9.3 Pre and post violence counts from Operation Thumbs Down

	Before the operation	During or after the operation
Activity area	229	208
Buffer area	265	233
Control area	483	452

so any trends in the city's crime patterns that would affect the activity area would also likely affect the control site, but it was also some distance from the activity site.

We counted the number of violent crimes in the three areas in the 14 months before the gang take-down, and the 14 months since the operation (Table 9.3). If you download the spreadsheet and plug in these numbers, you will see that crime in the control area reduced by 6 percent; however, it was reduced by 9 percent in the activity area where the gang interdiction occurred. The operation had a modest benefit and made the community a little safer. There was a larger benefit to the area where the task force officers thought crime might displace. That area actually had a diffusion of benefits. These reductions may seem modest, but realistic expectations are important (especially in the public service!). Hot spots policing is among the most reliable policing tactics evaluated, but as shown in Chapter 6, it generally results in modest crime reductions. There are no silver bullets out there.

Even if you do not have a buffer area as part of your operational strategy, you can still use the spreadsheet to calculate whether you have been a success. Uncheck the box for buffer counts and read off the results for non-buffer operations.

CHAPTER SUMMARY

• The OILRIG checklist is designed to help you reveal what worked, what didn't, and how you might improve components of your crime reduction strategy.

- An outcome evaluation examines what success and accomplishments the program generated and will tell you whether you were effective in achieving your outcome goals.
- A process evaluation determines whether program activities have been implemented as intended and if you got the outputs you expected.
- One way to determine the next stage is to conduct a post-mortem of your strategy.
- The ABC spreadsheet requires before and after counts of crime or disorder in Activity, Buffer, and Control areas and can help evaluate your strategy.

NOTE

* Scared Straight is a largely discredited program that aimed to deter at-risk juveniles from committing crime through prison tours involving confrontational and aggressive presentations by inmates designed to demonstrate the horrors of prison life. Extensive research has shown that the program did not reduce the likelihood that juveniles in the program will commit offenses in the future.

REFERENCES

1   Boon, B., Blackstone's Leadership for Sergeants and Inspectors. 2015, Oxford: Oxford University Press.

2   Maple, J. and C. Mitchell, The Crime Fighter: Putting the Bad Guys out of Business. 1999, New York: Doubleday.

3   Syed, M., Black Box Thinking: Why Most People Never Learn from Their Mistakes—But Some Do. 2015, New York: Portfolio/Penguin.

4   Ratcliffe, J.H., A. Perenzin, and E.T. Sorg, Operation Thumbs Down: A quasi-experimental evaluation of an FBI gang takedown in South Central Los Angeles. Policing: An International Journal of Police Strategies and Management, 2017. **40**(2): p. 442–58.

10

EVIDENCE-BASED POLICING

POLICING AS A SCIENCE

I recently witnessed an illustrative lesson. A number of senior managers were pitching an idea to their commander. It required the redistribution of patrols, but they were armed with evidence that the existing beats weren't in good locations and were ineffective. The commander sat back in his chair and said: "So I have to move some of those patrols?" "Yes," the managers replied, but responded with a cogent and measured presentation based on a thorough data analysis supported with current academic research. I thought they made an excellent case. The commander replied: "Well *in my experience*, those patrols *are* being effective so I am not going to move them." And at that point the meeting ended. In policing it's not just the case that culture eats strategy for breakfast: what passes for experience seems to eat data, science, and evidence.

Policing is unique in the discretion and absence of supervision given to the least experienced officers. As a teenager starting in patrol, I can testify to the steep learning curve on entering the job. Experiences come at you thick and fast. We mostly learn from these experiences. Most cops quickly absorb how to speak with people who are drunk or emotionally disturbed in a way that doesn't end up in them rolling around in the street with fists flying. My colleagues demonstrated a style and tone and I learned from the experience they had gained over time. But in the 21st century, professions do not advance by experience alone.

In the preface to his famous 1796 *Treatise on the Police of the Metropolis*, Patrick Colquhoun wrote: "Police in this country may be considered a new science; the properties of which consist not in the judicial powers which lead to punishment, and which belong to magistrates alone; but in the prevention and detection of crimes."[1] Today, the application of science to the prevention and detection of crimes, as well as improvements in the policing function generally, can be found in evidence-based policing.

It has long been argued that policing is a craft. But the rise of evidence-based policing has brought more focus on what constitutes evidence and knowledge of good practice. The aim is to supplement the craft of policing with some of the scientific principles that have moved so many other avenues of human endeavor forward. At the very least, as so succinctly tweeted by astrophysicist Neil deGrasse Tyson: "To be scientifically literate is to empower yourself to know when someone else is full of shit."

Evidence-based policing has been described as the "use of the best available research on the outcomes of police work to implement guidelines and evaluate agencies, units, and officers"[2] but more recently a preferred definition has emerged from the U.K. College of Policing (see Box 10.1).

BOX 10.1 WORKING DEFINITION OF EVIDENCE-BASED POLICING

According to the U.K. College of Policing's working definition, "in an evidence-based policing approach, police officers and staff create, review and use the best available evidence to inform and challenge policies, practices and decisions."[3]

What makes the definition in Box 10.1 useful is that the stress is on police to generate the evidence they can use. As scholar Egon Bittner wrote "It is clearly not for lawyers, sociologists, or psychologists to develop an intellectually credible version of what police work should be like. This must be left to scholarly policemen, just as the analogous task is left to scholarly physicians, social workers, or engineers."[4] A growing number of police practitioners who also embrace academic learning—known as pracademics—are at the center of a push for police to generate more evidence on their role in society. Pracademics are people who are both academics engaged in research and publishing, and active police officers.

Pracademics are people who are both academics engaged in research and publishing, and active police officers.

Having an evidence basis for what we do has many advantages. It can test the assumptions we might have about what causes crime and other problems. We can also avoid doing activities that have been shown not to work (such as Scared Straight and Drug Abuse Resistance Education, a school-based drug use education prevention course that has consistently been shown to not reduce the use of alcohol and drugs). Evidence can be an effective way to persuade politicians and the public, and in times of fiscal constraint improve the delivery of service to the community. It can even be an antidote to HIPPO policing, that is, policing based on the **Hi**ghest **P**aid **P**erson's **O**pinion. Science and research can distinguish between good intentions and good programs.

It's challenging to be a full-time police officer and a full-time academic and you may not have the time. So, what do you need to know to get by? What will help you make best use of what science tells us about policing? And how do you integrate that with your experience? The answers to these questions are the subject of this chapter, and arguably a thread throughout the whole book. Let's start by looking at the pros—and cons—of various types of evidence and experience.

EVIDENCE AND EXPERIENCE

Four types of evidence useful in policing

In the policy world, not all research evidence is created equally. I'm not talking here about forensic or criminal evidence. I'm referring to the evidence you need to make the best possible policy choice. It's not just about 'what works' to reduce crime significantly, but also *how* it works (what mechanism is taking place) and *when* it works (in what contexts the tactic may be effective).

We can harvest ideas about what might work from a variety of sources. Cody Telep and Cynthia Lum found that a library database was the *least* accessed source for officers when learning about what tactics might work.[5] That might be because for most police officers, a deep dive into the academic literature is like being asked to do foot patrol in Hades while wearing a nylon ballistic vest. But it also means that the 'what, how, and when works' of crime reduction are never fully understood. Too many cops unfortunately rely on their intuition, opinion, or unreliable sources. As Ken Pease and Jason Roach[6] write: "Collegiality among police officers is an enduring feature of police culture. . . . When launching local initiatives, their first action tends to be the arrangement of visits to similar initiatives in other forces, rather than taking to the journals."

In fact, not only do officers favor information from other cops, but it also has to be from the *right* police officers. Just about everyone in policing has, at some point, been told to forget what they learned at the police academy, even though academy instructors are usually fellow police officers. It's simply too easy to end up with a very narrow range of experiences on which to draw.

Researchers in evidence-based management argue that practitioners should consider evidence from four different types of sources, adapted for policing in Table 10.1.[7]

Table 10.1 Types of evidence relevant to police decision-making

Scientific evidence	Scientific research is usually published in academic journals and books. In recent years, there has been an explosion of research into policing. You can also find relevant studies in some government and agency reports. Learn how to assess the quality of these studies.
Organizational evidence	Police departments record a huge volume of data that are rarely analyzed, yet can provide significant insight. These include not just crime and arrest data but also reports from investigative interviews and victim surveys. Organizational problems can be better understood with employee information, financial breakdowns, internal affairs records, and sickness reports.
Professional evidence	The tacit understanding of problems that officers and detectives build up over time can be used to provide insights where hard (digital) data are lacking. Officers—especially those in a specialized role for a period of time—can reflect on their wealth of experiences to extract meaningful lessons that can help when tackling problems and implementing solutions.
Stakeholder evidence	Stakeholders can create a context for analyzing the other forms of evidence. Any person or group that is likely to be affected by the outcome of your project can be a stakeholder. They can be internal to the police service or an external partner. Understanding their values and concerns can help you avoid implementation problems and pushback. Incorporating what stakeholders find important can make the difference in long-term projects.

Collating evidence from all four sources is an important stage in broadening your decision-making and moving away from risking a subjective call based just on your opinion. Different circumstances will determine how much weight you put into each category. At the least, the process of going through information and data gathering from each of these will indicate to stakeholders and your colleagues that their views are being considered. Most area commanders appear to favor professional expertise over the other sources, but it has its strengths and weaknesses.

Collating evidence from all four sources is an important stage in broadening your decision-making and moving away from risking a subjective call based just on your opinion.

What role for experience?

When learning to be a pilot I heard an old flying aphorism. Good decisions come from experience, and experience comes from bad decisions. This quote (sometimes replacing decisions with judgment) is attributed to various sources, but the most common is Mark Twain. It's appropriate for flying, and my fondness for checklists stems from the aviation industry's use of them to reduce the poor decision-making spiral. Unfortunately, while it would be nice if new recruits could learn from their bad decisions, our modern intolerance for honest mistakes and anything-but-perfection precludes this. Therefore, how do we develop and grow a culture of good decisions? And what is the role of experience?

In praise of experience

The evidentiary foundation for much of policing is currently rather thin. For many areas, we do not yet know much about what good practice looks like. The UK College of Policing notes that: "Where there is little or no formal research, other evidence such as professional consensus and peer review, may be regarded as the 'best available.'" So practitioner judgment may help fill a void until that time when we have more research across a wider variety of policing topics. In time, this research will help officers achieve better practice. In the meantime, shared experience may be of value, if—in the words of the College of Policing—"gathered and documented in a careful and transparent way."

Personal intuition and opinion may not be a sound basis on which to make policy, but sometimes it can offer insights in rarely studied areas. This can prompt new ways of looking at problems. By varying experience, we can learn new ways to deal with issues. These new ways could then be tested more formally. There is definitely a place for personal judgment in the craft of policing, but overreliance on it prevents us embracing a culture of curiosity and developing the evidence base.

> There is definitely a place for personal judgement in the craft of policing, but overreliance on it prevents us embracing a culture of curiosity and developing the evidence base.

A critique of personal experience

Like the commander at the start of this section, unfortunately, most police leaders don't make decisions using the best evidence available. They overwhelmingly prefer decisions that are entrenched in their personal experience. But everyone's experience is limited (we can't have been everywhere and dealt with every type of incident). A Philadelphia patrol officer will report quite a few burglaries, but only a tiny fraction of the more than 5,000 committed each year. In some of the first research I completed, we discovered even experienced police officers are not great at identifying crime hot spots (they are better at some crime types than others)[8] and they do not do as well as a computer algorithm.[9]

As cops, even with many years under our belt, we generally receive too little feedback to learn potentially vital lessons. For example, as a young probationer, I attended countless domestic disturbance calls armed with so little personal experience in long-term relationships it was laughable. But the measure of 'success' (against which 'experience' was judged) was if we got a call back during that shift. If we did, I had failed. If we didn't, I was on my way to gaining the moniker of 'experienced.'

But what if the man beat his partner to within an inch of her life after my shift had gone home? Or the next week? If we weren't on duty I would never learn that my mediation attempts had been unsuccessful or worse, harmful. Without this feedback, I would probably continue to deal with domestic disturbance calls in the same way. Absent a visibly negative reaction, not only would I continue to act in a harmful manner, but my colleagues might think I was now 'experienced.' They might prioritize my attendance at these calls, and perhaps eventually give me a field training role. My bad practice would now become established 'good' policy.

As others have noted, "personal judgment alone is not a very reliable source of evidence because it is highly susceptible to systematic errors."[7] This isn't just an issue for policing—it's a human trait. Experts, many with years of experience, are often poor at making forecasts across a range of businesses and professions. The doctors that continued to engage in blood-letting into the latter half of the 19th century weren't being callous. They probably had good intentions. But their well-meaning embrace of personal judgment, tradition, and supposed best practice (probably learned from a medical 'expert') killed people.

> I describe a range of crime prevention interventions and ask which are effective. It's rare to find anyone who can get the correct answer, and most people are wildly off target.

When I lead training on evidence-based and intelligence-led policing, I often run a quick test. I describe a range of crime prevention interventions and ask which are effective. It's rare to find anyone who can get the correct answer, and most people are wildly off target. It illustrates how training and education in policing still remains at odds with a core activity, the reduction in crime and disorder.

When we are expected to use our experience so frequently, we come to think of it as infallible and don't seek out different approaches. We become prisoners of our experience.

A role for professional experience?

As Barends and colleagues note,[7] "Different from intuition, opinion or belief, professional experience is accumulated over time through reflection on the outcomes of similar actions taken in similar situations." It differs from personal experience because professional experience pools the knowledge of many practitioners. It also emerges from explicit reflection on the outcomes of actions. Without reflection we can too easily rely on information that is more recent or observed personally (what researchers call the availability bias) or cherry-pick information that fits our assumptions and beliefs (confirmation bias).

This explicit reflection requires feedback. When I was learning to land airplanes, a jarring sensation and the sound of the instructor wince was the immediate feedback I needed to tell me I had 'arrived' instead of landed! This type of immediate opportunity to improve by observing the effects of our decisions is rare in policing. The radio has already dragged us to another call.

For many enforcement activities, a research evaluation is therefore essential to provide the kind of feedback that you can't get from personal observation. The research on foot patrols and local violence is a good example of how research evidence can improve strategy and increase public safety. Science and evaluation can incorporate the experiences of hundreds of practitioners and pool that wisdom. While one officer can walk a single foot beat and think it's a waste of time, the aggregate experiences and data from 240 officers across 60 beats told us differently during the Philadelphia Foot Patrol Experiment.[10]

Tapping into scientific research findings and available organizational data (such as crime hot spot maps) and temporal charts will enhance our professional experience. Being open to the possibility that our intuition and personal opinion may be flawed is also important, though challenging. And developing a culture of curiosity that embraces trying new ways of tackling crime and disorder problems might be the most important change of all.

UNDERSTANDING RESEARCH STUDIES

Fortunately, while a basic understanding of different research qualities is helpful, you do not need to have an advanced degree in research methodology to be able to implement evidence-based policing. It's sufficient to appreciate that there is a hierarchy of evidence in which to place your trust, and to have a rudimentary understanding of the differences. I'm not dismissing any forms of research, but I am suggesting that some research is more reliable and useful for operational decision-making. In my own studies, a mix of approaches that combines quantitative and qualitative research has been useful for understanding why projects were successful or not. While the number-crunching will tell us *what* happened, the qualitative interviews and surveys can sometimes explain *why*.

For rigorous methodological studies, researchers look to fulfil four criteria, as shown in Box 10.2. Without a *plausible mechanism* to explain how an intervention reduced crime, we can end up with spurious correlations that make no sense. As I noted earlier in the book, in many places violence increases in the summer, but so do ice-cream sales. Having a plausible theory stops us jumping to the conclusion that sweet frozen treats turn us into homicidal maniacs.

We also want to see *temporal causality* where crime starts to decline after an intervention started (note though that publicity can sometimes cause anticipatory effects). *Statistical association* is important because we want to be sure any differences or findings are not potentially the result of random fluctuation in crime. Finally, good research does its best to *reject competing explanations* for any crime drop, such as changes in neighborhood demographics or Vanilla Magnum consumption. If a study can address all of these components, then it is likely to be taken more seriously by researchers and pracademics.

> ## BOX 10.2 FOUR COMPONENTS OF METHODOLOGICALLY RIGOROUS EVALUATIONS
>
> A plausible mechanism
> Temporal causality
> Statistical association
> Reject competing explanations

Criminologists are familiar with the Maryland Scientific Methods Scale devised by Larry Sherman and his colleagues.[3] In this scale, studies are ranked from 1 (weak) to 5 (strong) based on the study's capacity to show causality and limit the effects of bias. The hierarchy in Figure 10.1 is adapted from this and other sources, and emphasizes strong quantitative studies and randomized trials. Some researchers argue that randomized trials can be of limited value, difficult or impossible to implement, and that observational studies and other sources of information can also inform policing.[11] After-action reports can also improve future operational practices, and analyses that involve qualitative approaches can inform specific policy areas. But if you have an opportunity to conduct a study, strive for the highest methodological quality you can achieve. A section later in the chapter describes where you can get help.

While there is a focus on academic research, police officers obtain knowledge and information from a range of sources. Go into any police canteen or break room and you hear anecdote after anecdote. These examples of homespun wisdom—also known as non-typical case studies—are often illustrative of an unusual case rather than a story of the mundane and ordinary that we deal with every day. Being memorable, they often reflect an availability bias rather than evidence of a particular trend, so anecdotes are at the bottom of the evidence hierarchy.

Always consider the source and the medium, and try to reflect on particular characteristics of the evidence.[12] First, check the *authenticity* of the authors and that they represent the agency or organization,

Study description	Example	Implication
5* Systematic review/ meta-analysis of quality studies	The totality of evidence from numerous rigorous studies supports hot spots policing as effective.	**What works** in the given context
5 Randomized controlled experiments	Randomly selected areas for foot beats had reduced crime versus comparable beat areas.	
4 Before/after across multiple sites or groups, or quality longitudinal analysis	Body-worn cameras reduced assaults on officers in multiple cities, compared to cities without.	**What's promising** and definitely worth examining with more rigorous studies
3 Before/after with one site and a comparison site/group	Violent crime reduced after a big gang take-down but was unchanged in a comparable gang area.	
2 Cross-sectional comparison of treatment and control, or before/ after of treatment alone	Crime decreased after a city started using automated license plate readers.	**What's interesting** but should be looked at further with better studies
1 One-off measure with no comparison site/group	Police districts with more Hispanic residents have less crime than other areas.	
0 Commercial or internal non-peer reviewed research and reports	A commercial company's positive evaluation of its own software product.	**What's suspect** if presented as the only source of evidence
0 Expert opinion, anecdotes, case studies	Police chief memoires, or quotes from academics in newspapers.	

Figure 10.1 Evidence hierarchy for policy decision-making

if that is important to your interpretation of their work. Second, do they have the credibility to write the report or make their statement? Are they qualified and working in an area in which they have expertise? Have they been honest in reporting any findings fully and transparently and been honest about any conflicts of interest? Has it been peer-reviewed? Then consider the representativeness and context of the report. Do the authors report on an unusual case or on a generalized case that is illustrative of a widespread trend? Both are important, but it might be useful to recognize that distinction. Is the context broadly relevant to your project? Finally, what is the real meaning to you of the report? Be clear about the key findings and explain why they are useful to your problem.

WHERE TO FIND EXISTING EVIDENCE

If you have a crime problem, where can you get help? A number of governments have websites where you can source the latest research findings. These sites are more than just warehouses for research. They have often taken the hard work out of wading through endless research reports and academic articles, and distilled the key findings down to more easily digestible summaries. Webmasters have a tendency to change their websites as soon as a book like this is published (out of spite?), so if you are unable to find the websites described below, check with the website for this book where you will find updated links.

The UK College of Policing Crime Reduction Toolkit

http://whatworks.college.police.uk/toolkit/

The Crime Reduction Toolkit uses the EMMIE framework to identify and summarize the best available research evidence on what works to reduce crime. It draws on systematic reviews of research, which are the strongest evidence (5*) in Figure 10.1. The EMMIE framework is a ranking system developed by researchers to examine more than just effectiveness. While having an *effect* on crime is vital, the framework also addresses what *mechanisms* and *moderators* are important, as well as *implementation* and *economic cost* implications (Box 10.4).

BOX 10.3 THE EMMIE FRAMEWORK

Effect	What was the impact on crime?
Mechanism	How is the intervention supposed to work?
Moderators	Where will it work, and not work?
Implementation	What do you need to consider to make it work?
Economic cost	How much will it cost?

At the time of writing, the toolkit reported on over 50 different types of intervention, from street lights to targeting asset forfeiture to reduce organized crime. It's an easy site to search.

Crime Solutions

www.crimesolutions.gov/programs.aspx

This National Institute of Justice (NIJ) website collates both programs and practices and reviews them against a simple scale of *effective, promising,* and *no effect. Programs* are detailed projects and activities that are implemented as a specific response to a problem. They are therefore specific to a place, time and context. That being said, they are useful and illustrative of many programs implemented across the United States and other countries.

Practices are the programs and strategies that you might employ, such as hot spots policing, street-level drug enforcement, or DUI checkpoints. The practices part of the website provides a useful summary after a balanced review of the various positive and/or negative evaluations. Note that when you access the site, it can take up to a minute or more for all of the programs and practices to load into your browser. An example of one study is the Philadelphia Policing Tactics Experiment, a collaboration between the Philadelphia Police Department and Elizabeth Groff, myself, and our colleagues. An abbreviated version of how Crime Solutions summarized the experiment is shown in Box 10.4.

BOX 10.4 ABBREVIATED SUMMARY OF THE PHILADELPHIA POLICING TACTICS EXPERIMENT

Program goals:

The Philadelphia Policing Tactics Experiment was a randomized controlled field experiment that tested three approaches to hot spots policing: offender-focused (OF) policing, foot patrol, and problem-oriented policing. OF policing is a deterrence-based strategy targeting high-risk offenders. Targeted offenders were identified by intelligence analysts. This tactic was implemented in 20 violent crime hot spots.

Program activities:

The selected individuals were subjected to increased police attention, including proactive questioning and surveillance.

Evaluation outcomes:

Groff and colleagues (2015) report that areas in Philadelphia that received OF policing experienced a statistically significant decrease in violent crime, with a 42 percent reduction in violent crime relative to the control areas that were patrolled as usual by police officers. In addition, there was a statistically significant decrease in violent felony crimes. Violent felony counts were 50 percent lower in the OF policing areas compared with the control areas. Ratcliffe and colleagues (2015) reported no statistically significant differences in how citizens residing in hot spots viewed crime and disorder in their area before and after OF policing was implemented.

Implementation information:

The OF component was introduced during a meeting with the Philadelphia Police Department executive command staff, district commanders, and officers assigned to implement OF strategies, and the police department's Central Intelligence Unit. To ensure that officers were complying with the OF components, researchers viewed officers' daily logs and incident reports to determine what activities they performed during the 12-week intervention. The incident reports provided lists of the repeat offenders that the officers were targeting and the number of times the targeted offenders were questioned.

This is an abbreviated project summary of the Crime Solutions website. For the full summary, see https://www.crimesolutions.gov/ProgramDetails.aspx?ID=449.

The Campbell Collaboration

www.campbellcollaboration.org

The Campbell Collaboration produces systematic reviews (graded 5* in the evidence hierarchy in Figure 10.1) across a range of social science areas. In the area of crime and justice, more than half of the reviews are policing interventions. The website contains the full reports with detailed explanations of each study included, but also has a number of useful plain language summaries. Included summaries cover restorative justice conferencing, legitimacy in policing, and deterring corporate crime.

The Evidence-Based Policing matrix

http://cebcp.org/evidence-based-policing/the-matrix

The Evidence-Based Policing matrix was developed by researchers at George Mason University's Center for Evidence-Based Crime Policy. The studies are categorized by a three-dimensional tool that summarizes police tactics on three axes: the type or scope of the target, the extent to which the strategy is proactive or reactive, and the specificity of the prevention mechanism.

As the website explains, the aim of the visual tool is to reveal "clusters of studies within intersecting dimensions, or 'realms of effectiveness.' These realms provide insights into the nature and commonalities of effective (or not effective) police strategies and can be used by police agencies to guide developing future tactics and strategies, or assessing their tactical portfolio against the evidence." While it can take a moment to get your head around the three dimensions of the matrix, the website has a number of supporting tools and videos to help you use the matrix and its studies.

The Center for Problem-Oriented Policing

www.popcenter.org

While unfortunately no longer funded by the U.S. government, the Center for Problem-Oriented Policing has long been a valuable source for information on a variety of policing subjects. Fortunately, a university continues to support the website. It contains over 70 problem-specific guides that are designed to give you everything you need to know about how to understand and combat a variety of problems. Topics range from elder abuse or robberies of pharmacies to traffic congestion and rave parties.

A dozen or so response guides are also available. These summarize the collective knowledge of field research and best practices and can tell you how, and under what contexts, a number of common responses to crime do or don't work. Summaries include CCTV (video surveillance), asset forfeiture, dealing with crime in urban parks, and police crackdowns. Finally, there are about a dozen documents that guide you through the process of understanding crime problems.

The Reducing Crime website

reducingcrime.com

The website that supports this book isn't designed as a repository of crime prevention evaluations but it does contain some useful summaries. It is also the place to visit if the links listed above do not work. Please check with this book's website for updated links, new sources, and other information.

BRINGING TOGETHER THE EVIDENCE

Faced with a crime problem, and at the part of the PANDA model where you have to nominate a strategy around VIPER, how should you pull together the evidence? Table 10.2 suggests a five-stage process for building evidence into your decision-making.

Let's check in on Amy, our area commander. A new problem scan and analysis of her *organizational evidence* (data) suggests she has a couple of emerging hot spot locations (crime spikes) that are active in the late evenings. When she *canvases stakeholders*, the community and businesses in the area ask for a juvenile curfew program. With a hypothesis testing approach (Chapter 7), she brings together some

Table 10.2 A process for building evidence into decision-making

Review organizational evidence	Review the organizational data that your police department has. This should have been done as part of your VOLTAGE analysis in the *Analyze problem* part of PANDA.
Canvas stakeholders	What are the perspectives of senior executives, street officers, partner agencies, and any other communities likely to be affected? This is your stakeholder evidence.
Gather professional expertise	What is the (often tacit) professional evidence available in your department? Collate various views and suggestions.
Collate scientific research	Visit the websites in this chapter and collate what is known about the problem you are tackling. Compare stakeholder opinions and professional experience against current scientific knowledge. If you have time, you can also contact societies for evidence-based policing, and local universities.
Weigh the evidence	Weigh the various pieces of evidence against your organizational capacities, external support, and situational context. Consider source authenticity, credibility, representativeness, context, and meaning to your crime problem. Try and coordinate possible solutions with VIPER components.

street and community officers who work the area. They tell her that they think that a few specific offenders are largely responsible. This adds to her *professional evidence*.

Finally, she reviews the *scientific evidence*. Her review of the websites listed in this chapter shows that juvenile curfews have not been shown to be effective for vehicle crime. She then reads that hot spots policing is generally effective, and that proactive patrolling of around 15 minutes every hour or two (what is called the Koper Curve) has been recognized as a possible approach. This might be possible in her organizational context because she can ask headquarters for some supporting resources to supplement her own officers. Her website research finds that street lights might also be effective.

Taking an evidence-based policing approach to parts of her VIPER strategy, she decides to integrate hot spot patrols as her enforcement (E in VIPER) approach, a push for improved street lights as a prevention mechanism (P in VIPER), and a program of publicity targeted at the local community as a reassurance policy (R in VIPER).

STARTING TO DEVELOP YOUR OWN EVIDENCE

Inevitably, you will at some point find a problem that does not have a relevant research background. Or you may find that the website tools listed in this chapter do not work in your area or in the particular context of your problem. This is where you can make a contribution to policing or even just learn a little more about what is effective by developing your own evidence. Renée Mitchell was a sergeant with the Sacramento (California, U.S.) police department when she became the first police officer to lead a randomized and controlled experiment in her own department (see Box 10.5). The Sacramento Hot Spots Experiment is now a well-known study.

> ### BOX 10.5 RUNNING A RESEARCH PROJECT IN THE POLICE SERVICE
>
> "In 2010, the Sacramento Police Department faced the financial reality of losing 50 police officers over the next year. The chief wanted to figure out how to do more with less, so my task as the crime analysis sergeant was to figure out how to use officers' time between calls for service more effectively. That same year I audited two weeks of a two-year police executive program at the University of Cambridge and discovered evidence-based policing. I knew about hot spots policing, but also learned we could test our predicament with a randomized controlled trial.

We needed to increase patrol effectiveness, so I designed a 90-day randomized experiment to see if a (Koper Curve) policy of 15-minute high visibility patrols at hot spots would help. University researchers helped with my understanding of good research design, the importance of vigorously supervising the implementation, and how to analyze the outcome data. I thought I would get some push back, but the Sacramento Hot Spot Experiment was borne from necessity and I confess I was surprised at how quickly my captains got on board. We needed to learn what worked for us, and it was conducted in short order in response to pending budgetary cuts and layoffs. The results were a 25% drop in serious crimes and a 7.7% drop in calls for service when compared to control hot spots."

Renée Mitchell is a sergeant in the Sacramento (CA) police department (U.S.). She has a PhD from the University of Cambridge and is currently the president of the American Society of Evidence-Based Policing.

There isn't the space in this short book to provide instruction on how to design and implement a fully-fledged research study; however, the *assess outcomes* (second A in PANDA) stage is one starting point. There are also other resources that you should seek out if you really want to make your mark on policing. Some are listed below, and don't forget to visit the website that supports this book for more information.

Academic and national institutions

Policing research was not a focus of academic study until recently, and many criminology and sociology university departments are still reluctant to engage with police in research projects. However, there are a number of criminal justice, crime science, policing, geography and other academic units across the globe that are increasingly interested in policing research and enthusiastic about helping you evaluate and improve policing. Look through the faculty lists of these departments at nearby universities. Seek out faculty who have previously worked with police or have useful research interests. Be prepared to be flexible. Policing researchers can have varied backgrounds yet still make a useful contribution, so look beyond criminology departments. You might find researchers who can help in geography, sociology, and even the physical sciences. Read their biographies online and see if they have skills and interests that are of use to you.

In some countries, national agencies support policing research. They may run workshops or conferences, have Twitter feeds worth following, or support police department research with grant funding. See the website that supports this book for details and links.

Evidence-based policing societies

A number of countries have evidence-based policing societies. Some of the main ones are in this section. The *Society of Evidence Based Policing* is based in the U.K. and runs an annual conference dedicated to evidence-based policing. The society is run by volunteers (such as Roger Pegram from Box 10.6) drawn from sworn officers, police staff, and academics.

BOX 10.6 A PERSONAL TIPPING POINT FOR EVIDENCE-BASED POLICING

"I had little in the way of education, but I had passed the detective and sergeant exams. I didn't really think universities could influence policing, but I enrolled in a degree at a local institution because I wanted a promotion! My former chief spoke about professionalization but it didn't mean much to me until I started to learn and consider what motivated people to commit crime, why people do what they do, how the criminal justice system worked, and most importantly my purpose and role in it. I realized that I had been following my training, standard operating procedures, and criminal law, but missing the point.

When you have a reflective experience like that you want to share it with others. I got involved with the Society of Evidence Based Policing in its formative year and set about educating people in my own force. The message was simple: this is about education not training, and about thinking critically and making informed decisions. We are creating a culture of curiosity and encouraging respectful challenge, ensuring that we are problem-solving, and working in the most efficient and effective ways to keep society safe. Within eight years of hearing my chief challenging us on professionalization I had two master's degrees and was a visiting scholar at the University of Cambridge. A regular cop was now hooked."

Roger Pegram is an inspector with Greater Manchester Police (U.K.) and vice chair of the Society of Evidence Based Policing.

The society has three aims. First, to increase use of best available research evidence to solve policing problems. Second, to encourage police practitioners and researchers to produce new research evidence. Third, to improve the communication of research evidence to police practitioners and the public. Their website has a number of resources and links, and can be found at sebp.police.uk.

The *Australia & New Zealand Society of Evidence Based Policing* (ANZSEBP) was formed in 2013 with the aim of making evidence-based methodology part of everyday policing in Australia and New Zealand. At their website (anzsebp.com) you can find various resources. Membership is free and allows members access to their journal as well as reduced subscriptions to conferences and journals.

The *American Society of Evidence Based Policing* (ASEBP) can be found at americansebp.com, where police volunteers maintain a blog for members and run a successful annual conference that brings together police practitioners with likeminded researchers.

The *Canadian Society of Evidence Based Policing* (CAN-SEBP) was formed in 2015 and also comprises police practitioners, academic researchers, public policy-makers, and others. Their website at can-sebp.net contains a number of videos and links to blog posts relevant to police practitioners everywhere and not just Canada.

CHAPTER SUMMARY

- In "an evidence-based policing approach, police officers and staff create, review and use the best available evidence to inform and challenge policies, practices, and decisions."
- Policing generally draws on four types of research evidence; scientific, organizational, professional, and stakeholder.
- Experience and intuition are useful to policing, especially in circumstances where there is little scientific evidence to guide best practice; however, intuition is vulnerable to biases and should be supplemented with research evidence where possible.
- Evidence has a hierarchy when applied to policy decision-making, with systematic reviews and randomized controlled trials being considered among the strongest evidence.
- A number of websites have been designed to help pracademics navigate the research literature on crime prevention and police tactics.

REFERENCES

1 Colquhoun, P., *A Treatise on the Police of the Metropolis*. 1796, London: J. Mawman.

2 Sherman, L.W., *Evidence-Based Policing*. 1998, Washington, D.C: Police Foundation.

3 U.K. College of Policing. *What is evidence-based policing?* 2017; Available from: http://whatworks.college.police.uk/About/Pages/What-is-EBP.aspx. Accessed 31st May 2018.

4 Bittner, E., *The Functions of the Police in Modern Society*. 1970, Rockville, MD: National Institute of Mental Health, Center for Studies of Crime and Delinquency.

5 Telep, C.W. and C. Lum, *The receptivity of officers to empirical research and evidence-based policing: An examination of survey data from three agencies*. Police Quarterly, 2014. **17**(4): p. 359–85.

6 Pease, K. and J. Roach, *How to morph experience into evidence* in *Advances in Evidence-Based Policing*, J. Knutsson and L. Tompson, Editors. 2017, Routledge: New York. p. 84–97.

7 Barends, E., D.M. Rousseau, and R.B. Briner, *Evidence-Based Management: The Basic Principles*. 2014, Amsterdam: Center for Evidence-Based Management.

8 Ratcliffe, J.H. and M.J. McCullagh, *Chasing ghosts? Police perception of high crime areas*. British Journal of Criminology, 2001. **41**(2): p. 330–41.

9 Weinborn, C., et al., *Hotspots vs. harmspots: Shifting the focus from counts to harm in the criminology of place*. Applied Geography, 2017. **86**: p. 226–44.

10 Ratcliffe, J.H. and E.T. Sorg, *Foot Patrol: Rethinking the Cornerstone of Policing*. 2017, New York: Springer (CriminologyBriefs).

11 Knutsson, J. and L. Tompson, *Introduction*, in *Advances in Evidence-Based Policing*, J. Knutsson and L. Tompson, Editors. 2017, Routledge: New York. p. 1–9.

12 Ratcliffe, J.H., *Intelligence research*, in *Strategic Thinking in Criminal Intelligence (2nd edition)*, J.H. Ratcliffe, Editor. 2009, Federation Press: Sydney. p. 108–23.

11

LEADERSHIP AND CRIME MANAGEMENT

A BRIEF PRIMER ON LEADERSHIP

Leadership is a rather nebulous concept. Leaders seem to have some inherent quality we recognize, either by their actions or characteristics. Leaders are able to inspire us, are strategic in their thinking, and can motivate and stimulate. Given the perpetual resource constraints and challenges in policing today, honesty with colleagues is also especially important. The leader's skill set has to be diverse and adaptive to circumstances, from strategic planning in seemingly endless meetings to on-the-ground leadership during high-stress incidents such as riots or fugitive searches. Leadership is also necessary in quieter times, such as when an officer has been involved in a police-involved shooting or needs to be counseled about the stresses associated with the job.

> Leaders are able to inspire us, are strategic in their thinking, and can motivate and stimulate.

It is nebulous because, for all this, it seems difficult to train people to be good leaders. Unlike technical skills that can be memorized, leadership is partly a function of character traits and what are sometimes called soft skills. Boon identifies a number of leadership styles.[1] For example, the *charismatic leader* has a certain force of personality—though there is little evidence that they are naturally a good leader. *Situational leaders* have the requisite skill set and qualifications, but often only for a particular situation. An *appointed leader* is selected and appointed based on merits and performance. Perhaps most usefully for policing, the *functional leader* can change approach to meet various demands and needs.

The challenge with policing is the sheer breadth of incidents and activities in which a leader will be involved. These skills have to be applied to not only the functional task of policing, but also to the development of the team and individual officers. This is the foundation for what John Adair called action-centered leadership.[2]

After serving in the Scots Guards, Adair became a senior lecturer in military history and leadership training at the British Royal Military Academy, Sandhurst. This is where I first came across his model. Beyond just a focus on task, he recognized that groups, like police units that you likely now command, can have personality and group needs. These include the need to accomplish a common task and to be a cohesive unit. The third component of his model is the needs of the individual members of the team (see Figure 11.1). Think about the group you command. It might be worth taking a moment to reflect on the needs of the individuals, the collective personality of the team, and how they go about achieving shared tasks.

This model is a simple primer, but there are many others. A visit to an airport bookshop will reveal endless alternative leadership models. You might want to review specific police leadership books or check whether your department advances a certain model. But for me, the appeal of Adair's model is its simplicity. The overlapping circles are indicative that even when you are strongly task focused, you have to consider the welfare of the individuals under your command as well as team cohesion and needs. As Adair notes: "these three areas of need influence each other for better or worse."

Figure 11.1 Adair's action-centered model

A good leader will adapt their leadership style depending on the circumstances. It's ideal to be in the center of the three circles; however, practicalities of policing sometimes necessitate a shift. Try and remember to return to a more centered leadership orientation when you can.

Leadership can be exercised in many ways. There is a tendency to think that the influence of a leader occurs in pressure situations, but a friend of mine, Police Chief Tom Nestel, has pointed out that the most influential tool in policing is the roll call podium. What is said at the start of the day by the supervisor sets the tone for all. Tone is not only set by the explicit actions of the leader, but also the implicit ones. As an example, Crawford and Cunningham argue that commendation ceremonies indicate what the organization values. They suggest that similar recognition should flow to those involved in challenging and "ingenious preventive partnerships."[3] Think about what you reward and recognize. Are you focused on public safety?

Does your focus represent the values you want your officers and subordinates to pursue? To quote Tom Nestel again, the 'running and gunning' aspect of policing certainly saves lives, but 'walking and talking' changes lives.

> The 'running and gunning' aspect of policing certainly saves lives, but 'walking and talking' changes lives.

To be transactional or transformational

In recent years, terms such as transactional and transformational leadership have crept into policing. In some ways, transactional leadership is suited to day-to-day managers. Leading in this style involves setting goals and using rewards and feedback to drive productivity. Transactional leaders tend to seek organizational efficiencies rather than challenge how the organization does business.

Transformational leadership engages with staff in more meaningful ways. These leaders think about organizational change and are big picture oriented. Transformational leaders are considered more inspirational, exhorting workers to perform beyond normal expectations, achieve more and seek aspirational goals for the benefits of others. A transformational leader is different from a transactional manager in a number of ways. A manager will focus on the immediate needs of the task, whereas a leader will keep a weather eye on the team and individual needs. Managers will still benefit from characteristics such as visibility and approachability, and should always strive to be open, fair, and honest. For leaders, these traits are vital.

While this description would tend to suggest everyone should be transformational leaders, the reality of police mid-level command suggests that you may need to adopt different positions depending on your officers and the circumstances. Some will be less experienced and will benefit from a clearer application of transactional authority on your part. There may also be times when urgency requires what some officers describe as a "task-not-ask" style.[4]

But experienced or more educated officers may be more satisfied and responsive if you move to the right on the continuum shown in Figure 11.2. This figure, adapted from Adair,[2] shows that as a commander moves from left to right, they adopt a different leadership style that will affect the team, the individual, and likely the task.

One component that is sometimes associated with a transformational leader is the concept of authenticity. An authentic leader is someone who exhibits a strong degree of self-awareness, is able to examine their own strengths and weaknesses, and possesses a strong team and an individual-centered, ethical foundation. Characteristics commonly associated with authentic leadership include showing genuine concern, being honest and consistent, and acting with integrity.

David Stewart drew on his experiences in Police Scotland to argue that when a program of change is needed "that is significantly timebound, and where clear progress needs to be delivered and maintained, a transformational approach through firm leadership will provide the best chance of success."[5] If you end up in a crisis and need a transactional, task-focused style, move to a focus on transformational team and individual development when the crisis dissipates.

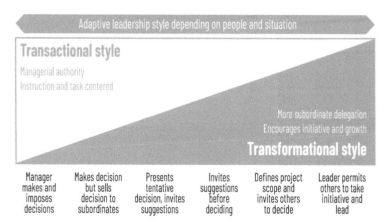

Figure 11.2 Leadership and decision-making continuum

Recognize also that this is a dynamic area and disagreements continue to circulate about the appropriate leadership style within policing. Check with your department's policy, if they have one.

MANAGING UP

If you are in the middle of the organization (in terms of rank), then you have to manage up as well as manage those officers that you command. Managing up sounds condescending, but it is a component of being a middle manager. You should have the best outcomes of the organization in mind, and how these outcomes maximize public benefit. Having an effective and productive relationship with your manager will be beneficial for both of you, as well as the citizens you serve. Here are some considerations.

What is it like in their shoes? As you move up the organization, you become increasingly exposed to the political pressures that challenge police leadership every day. Special interest groups, the community, and political groups, as well as rank-and-file police organizations and unions all want to pull the organization in a direction that suits their specific group. Take a moment to appreciate the various positions and challenges facing your boss.

> Transparency in police decision-making goes a long way. You may not like all of the choices that are made, but equally you may not be party to all of the information that went into a decision. Loyalty shouldn't be blind, but neither should it be absent.

Having just read about leadership styles, what style does your boss exhibit? If you can understand their leadership style, you can better situate yourself to respond to their needs and be able to negotiate mutually beneficial arrangements. Do they prefer face-to-face meetings, or dispense orders via email? Are they open to discussions in more public meetings or feel vulnerable and threatened when new ideas are advanced? Understanding their leadership style (and limitations) will help you better navigate your relationship.

Don't play office politics or engage in pejorative Machiavellian schemes. There is an unfortunately long history of police departments that had cliques and 'in' groups. They often ended up damaging the organization. Be supportive and positive, though realistic. Stay professional and fair, and avoid showing favoritism. Transparency in police decision-making goes a long way. You may not like all of the choices that are made, but equally you may not be party to all of the information that went into a decision. Loyalty shouldn't be blind, but neither should it be absent.

Try and keep your executive focused on long-term issues and out of the day-to-day micromanagement of the police service. Most of them were street cops at one point, and their instinct is often to wade into the weeds. Try and remind them their job is above the fray. They should steer, not row.

MANAGING ACROSS AND DOWN

As well as managing up, recognize that you also have to manage across and down. This means managing people at your level elsewhere in your organization as well as people in partnerships with whom you collaborate. Within the police service, you may be familiar with the culture of other units, but unfamiliar with the goals and perspectives of non-government agencies.

Cross-agency partnerships and collaborations open up new avenues for success but also challenges. Outside personnel often have different goals that do not necessarily complement your objectives. Sometimes they may be at odds with you, and the people from the other agencies may feel threatened. It's useful to recognize that their perspective makes sense—to them. Their personal and organizational metrics for success may clash with your crime reduction goal, or they may fail to see the merits of your plan and actively push back against it. They may not think they are being obstructive, but rather perceive their role as being helpful and clarifying.

A starting point to resolve these issues is to listen and take time to actively appreciate their perspective. You don't have to agree with their position, but if you take the time to try and understand why they might feel like they do, you can gain an understanding of how to move your agenda forward. Sometimes, their objections are simply founded in a resistance to change, and listening to their concerns will help you understand where the resistance is focused. Causes for resistance include:

- symbolic fears (a concern that they will lose status or power)
- uncertainty (worry that change will cause emotional stress and anxiety)
- competence fears (worry that they will not be able to do the new requirements)
- inconvenience (a concern that changes will be disruptive)
- the shock of the new (an unwillingness to step out of a comfort zone).

These are just a number of possible causes for resistance to change;[1,6] however, spending time listening to the other party will give you useful insights into working with them.

It is also worth reflecting for a moment on this list. Are these symptoms that you are vulnerable to? Do these challenges prevent you from embracing new ideas?

Delegation

You are going to have to delegate some of your responsibilities as an area commander. This is inevitable, because you won't have the time necessary to achieve all of the tasks you take on or are assigned. Delegation will help you manage your stress levels, develop your team, tap into expertise you don't have, and your team will have more respect for a leader that confers some responsibilities on them (see Box 8.3 on page 156).

BOX 11.1 CONSIDERATIONS WHEN DELEGATING
RESPONSIBILITY

When delegating responsibility to another person, a good leader will
convey to the individual or consider the following:

- authority deferred should be clear to individuals
- conditions and limits of the delegation
- reasons for the delegation
- offer support to the individual
- monitor progress and/or request regular feedback
- praise individual if successful
- share credit
- remember that accountability cannot be delegated.

As with the deployment of your operation, try and seek individual
accountability with tasks that are assigned to subordinates or people in partnership organizations. Cognitive loafing (see Chapter 9)
is reduced when people think there is direct accountability. You
should also be clear about what authority is being delegated, the
conditions under which delegation is taking place, the reasons why
you are delegating to the individual, and provide support if needed.
Once under way, monitor their progress, and if they succeed in the
task offer praise and encouragement. There's often too little of this
going around. Delegation involves some risk on your part, so it is
appropriate to share some of the credit, but always remember that
accountability remains with you (see Box 11.1).[1]

Be a mentor and set the tone

Poor supervision is often blamed for lack of implementation success. Remember that in most police departments, people are not
promoted for their supervisory ability. It is usually based on their
aptitude to pass an exam and regurgitate legal statutes and standard

operating practices at the right time. We constantly have to work on our leadership skills, and so might the supervisors that work for you.

In the absence of evidence of ability, too often we respect time served. And while this experience can be a valuable commodity, it can also breed a certain solidifying of perspective. Earlier in this chapter, the importance of the roll call podium was mentioned, recognition of the importance of frontline supervisors in setting the tone for an entire shift. Any supervisors who report to you can support or undermine your initiatives. So, pay attention to the tone that you set, and that your supervisors set to your officers. Actively manage the attitude at your police station and don't assume your officers will buy into your plans. You should regularly reach out to them directly to get their full commitment (see Box 11.2).

BOX 11.2 ENCOURAGE AND TRAIN YOUR OFFICERS TO SWIM

"We needed to focus on the gang cliques in Santa Ana, but our agents (Salvadorian frontline officers) were not invested. Traditionally we brief the chiefs about new projects, but never the agents. We don't explain our plans, yet they are doing the work. We just issue orders.

Unfortunately, our agents were not completing field contact cards. I had to have the police take on the project as their own, yet as commissioner, there are about six ranks between me and my frontline agents. So, I speak directly to them. It's unusual. Many senior officers haven't been taught to manage power, and they think they know it all. We need more humility.

I explained to the agents what it was all about. We needed to change the mentality. It was vital to tell them about the importance of the project so they gave us real facts, not made-up information. It's also important to me that the agents have the same knowledge as their supervisors, so I speak directly to everyone. After all, the agents in some areas know more than their chiefs because of their experience. This is why we need to hear their opinions.

If our officers do the work properly, this is my success. I also offer incentives where I can. If they seize guns, we give them a few hours off, or a day if they arrest a dangerous criminal. The agents are the stars, but we also have to train them. You can't throw someone into a pool if they don't know how to swim."

Julio César Marroquín Vides is a commissioner (comisionado) in El Salvador's National Civil Police (PNC) currently supervising a national intelligence-led policing project.

RETHINK MANAGEMENT MEETINGS

If we are to promote more thoughtful and evidence-based policing, then in many agencies the crime management meeting process has to change. The Compstat-type crime management gathering has its origins in Bill Bratton's need to extract greater accountability from NYPD precinct commanders in late 1990s New York. It was innovative for the time and spawned many initiatives that are hugely beneficial to modern policing (such as the growth of crime mapping). Arguably, it has also been successful in promoting greater responsiveness from middle managers; however, these days the flaws are increasingly apparent (see Box 11.3).

BOX 11.3 A COMMANDER'S FIRST EXPERIENCE WITH COMPSTAT

"A few years ago, I was promoted to a Divisional Commander role. This placed me responsible for a specific geographical area and its overall patrol operations. We employ a Compstat model using a three-week planning cycle. Sadly, I arrived at my first meeting having never

been to a meeting before. I was never adequately briefed on expectations or educated on how Compstat functioned in conjunction with
our other units. I was also expected to report upward at a senior level.
Expected to chair and champion the Compstat process in my new
position, I felt totally unarmed.

Other officers were no different. We were all ill-prepared, there
was little direction and support to solve problems, and the word
Compstat often elicited eye rolling. There was no accountability or
ownership, and it showed with high crime trends. Compstat was a
lather, rinse, and repeat cycle with little meaning or effectiveness and
therefore little buy-in. The situation drove me bananas."

*Don Moser is currently an inspector and the opera-
tional planning officer for the Halifax Regional
Police, Nova Scotia, Canada.*

Over my years of watching Compstat-type meetings in many
departments, I've observed everyone settle into their Compstat role
relatively comfortably. Well almost. The mid-level local commander
who has to field questions is often a little uneasy, but these days few
careers are damaged in Compstat. A little preparation, some confidence, and a handful of quick statistics or case details to bullshit
through the tough parts will see a shrewd commander escape
unscathed.

The executives also know their role. They stare intently at the map,
ask about a crime hot spot or two, perhaps interrogate a little on a
case just to check the commander has some specifics on hand, and
then volunteer thoughts on a strategy the commander should try—
just to demonstrate their experience. One wit on Twitter calls it the

'Daily Hindsight meeting.' It's an easy role for the executives because it doesn't require any preparation. In turn, the area commander pledges to increase patrols in the neighborhood and everyone commits to reviewing progress next month, safe in the knowledge that little review will actually take place, because by then new dots will have appeared on the map to absorb everyone's attention. It's a one-trick pony and everyone is comfortable with the trick.

There are some glaring problems with this Compstat model. The first is that the analysis is weak and often just based on a map of dots or, if the department is adventurous, crime hot spots. A map of crime hot spots should be the *start* of an analysis, not the conclusion. It's great for telling us what is going on, but this sort of map can't really tell us *why*. We need more information and intelligence to get to why. And why is vital if we are to implement a successful crime reduction strategy.

When commanders have to magically create a response on the fly, the result is often a superficial enforcement choice.

We never get beyond this basic map because of the second problem: the frequent push to make an operational decision immediately. When commanders have to magically create a response on the fly, the result is often a superficial enforcement choice. Nobody wants to appear indecisive, but with crime control it can be disastrous. Too few commanders ever request more time to do additional analysis, or a pause to consider the evidence base for their strategies. I concede that tackling an emerging crime spike might be valuable (though they often regress to the mean/mediocrity). Most Compstat issues however revolve around chronic, long-term problems where a few days isn't going to make much difference. It's better to have a successful strategy next week than a failing one today.

Because of the pressure to miracle a working strategy out of thin air, area commanders usually default to a narrow set of standard approaches. Saturation patrol with uniform resources is the one I see more than 90 percent of the time. And it's applied to everything, regardless of whether there is any likelihood that it will impact the problem. It is suggested by executives and embraced by local area commanders because it is how we've always escaped from Compstat. Few question saturation patrols because it's a non-threatening, traditional policing approach. It's like a favorite winter coat, except that we like to wear it all year round.

Third, in the absence of a more thoughtful and evidence-based process, too many decisions lack any evidential support and instead are driven by personal views. Most Compstat meetings are reminiscent of the scene in the movie *Moneyball*, where all of the old baseball scouts are commenting on which players the team should buy, based on the scouts' experience, opinion, and personal judgment. They ignore the nerd in the corner who has real data and figures . . . and some insight. In the movie, the data analyst is disparaged because he hasn't been in baseball for more than five minutes, even though he doesn't bring an opinion to the table. He brings data analysis, and the data don't care how long you have been in the business.

A strategic and tactical Compstat

The problems with Compstat are weak analysis, rushed decision-making, and opinion-driven strategies. Where might a solution lie?

The U.K.'s National Intelligence Model is worth considering. After a lengthy review, the developers created both a strategic and a tactical cycle. The strategic meeting attendees determine the main strategic aims and goals for the district. This is important because as a senior commander told me "We are usually too busy putting out fires to care about who is throwing matches around". Any process that can strategically focus the tactical day-to-day management of a district has the capacity to retain at least one eye on the match throwers. A quarterly meeting (or at most monthly), focused on chronic district problems, can generate a handful of strategic priorities. You can draw these priorities from the chronics, spikes, and panics list developed in Chapter 2.

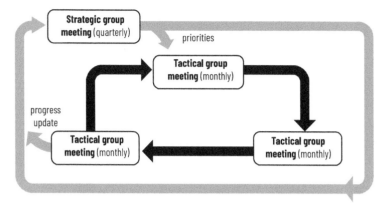

Figure 11.3 Strategic and tactical meeting cycle example

A more frequent tactical meeting is then tasked with implementing these strategic priorities. The tactical meeting shouldn't set strategic goals—that is the role of the strategic working group. The tactical meeting might be a monthly or bi-weekly gathering that can both deal with the dramas of the day as well as drive implementation of the goals set at the strategic meeting. The tactical meeting should always spend some time on the implementation of the larger strategic goals. In this way, the strategic goals are not subsumed by day-to-day dramas that often comprise the tyranny of the moment.

I've previously written that Compstat has become a game of 'whack-a-mole' policing with no long-term value.[7] Consider the structure in Figure 11.3 and if it could be applied to your area. Adjust the time frames if necessary (see book's website for other options). Remember that long-term chronic problems are not likely to be solved by inherited tactics and pre-existing approaches. They have all been tried. A focused and concentrated analytical effort is needed. If we don't retain a strategic eye on long-term goals, it's not effective policing. It's *Groundhog Day* policing.

MAKING AREA CHANGE HAPPEN

Prior to writing this book, I took a sabbatical and spent months in meetings and training with command staff from a number of countries. What follows are a few general management thoughts passed on by these leaders.

Don't kill all the cubs

When a new lion takes over the pride, they tend to kill all the cubs that were fathered by the previous male. As Ken Pease and Jason Roach point out, the lion doesn't want to waste time raising cubs that were not his. We often see the same thing in politics . . . and policing. Pease and Roach note, "Ambitious senior police officers will set their stall out for promotion by doing new things rather than consolidating old things."[8] As a new area commander, don't try and change everything immediately. The way things are done might not make sense initially, but they make sense to the people who lived through the previous change, and they made sense to your predecessor. When you kill the cubs unnecessarily, or even just let them wither, you can lose staff through retirement or just plain frustration, as witnessed by Pease and Roach. This isn't an argument for inertia, but rather an argument for data-driven change. Use the processes in this book to think through the various ramifications and create a decision-making system for the entire business of area command.

Procedural justice and legitimacy

Since the 1960s, innovative agencies have recognized the importance of public trust and confidence in the police. These ideas stem not from our ability to control crime, but instead from how people *experience* policing. Procedural justice emphasizes the nature of police interactions and how police treat the public during everyday encounters and normal police work. The idea is that when police behave in fair and considerate ways, they are demonstrating a recognition of the other person's dignity. In doing so, even when officers arrest an individual, the process is viewed as less objectionable. This establishes police legitimacy, a belief that police are entitled to operate in a community and use their authority to preserve social order, resolve conflicts, and solve problems. The theory is that when people believe that the police are behaving legitimately, they are "more inclined not only to defer to police authority in the present instance but also to collaborate with police in the future, even to the extent of being more inclined not to violate the law."[9]

Law enforcement operations that are driven by crime spikes tend to emphasize crackdowns in their attempt to get crime back under control. Over-enthusiastic enforcement can win the battle but lose the war. Crime comes down, but at the cost of community support. Reminding officers of the key tenets of procedural justice (Box 11.4) can help everyone maintain a sense of perspective.

First, police should give a *voice* to the public and allow them to tell their side of the story. Even if they are getting a ticket, people still want to feel like they have had their say and that at least some consideration has been given to their opinion. Second, the public want to feel that police are acting with *neutrality*, and the process is fair and consistent. Interestingly, the public can feel that the outcome of an interaction with the police can be fair, even if they still come out of it badly (say by being arrested). Third, police should demonstrate *trustworthy motives* surrounding the decision that the officer makes, even if it is to issue a ticket or make an arrest. The public would like to feel that the outcome of their situation is made with benevolence and the best outcomes for the community in mind. Last,

---

BOX 11.4 THE FOUR COMPONENTS OF PROCEDURAL JUSTICE

Give the public a *voice*
Act *neutrally*
Demonstrate *trustworthy motives*
Treat people with *dignity and respect*

treating people with *dignity and respect* is a central tenet of policing. It is believed that these 'four pillars' of procedural justice are linked to improvements in perceptions of police legitimacy.[9,10]

Don't be a policy weathervane

Some initiatives take time to mature, but if you don't maintain a focus on them, then they tend to wither and die. Be specific about your goals and don't suddenly change direction in response to the latest news article. Try and resist pressure to change strategies or resource allocations before they have had a chance to be effective. This is especially the case for work that integrates with partnerships, such as testing out different ways to resolve cases for low-level offenders, and other community programs. If you anticipate long implementation and learning times, you should set realistic timelines to monitor progress.

Police chiefs often attend national meetings with the hope of finding the next silver bullet; the next great initiative that will solve their crime and disorder problems and magically overcome the effects of years of underfunding of police and other social services. That silver bullet doesn't exist. To use an American football analogy, improvements in policing will not come from a trick play or a 'Hail Mary' pass all the way down the field. With the limited resources available to most police services, change will come from modest, incremental improvements. As American football coach Woody Hayes is credited with saying, they will be hard-earned over "three yards and a cloud of dust." That is harder to achieve when priorities change too often.

Avoid innovation-killing phrases

When I lead crime analysis training, I encourage analysts to always make recommendations to their leaders. This doesn't mean that their boss has to accept the recommendation. Far from it! But at least it gives them options, as long as the leaders are willing to listen to suggestions. We probably all have stories of leaders who had closed minds. One sergeant told me about spending, on the orders of his boss, weeks preparing an evaluation of a proposed change in operational policing. He finally had an opportunity to present his assessment, but before he said a word was told "I've made up my mind—don't baffle me with facts."

There are numerous other phrases that are commonly heard around police stations that can kill innovation:

- "We tried it and it doesn't work."
- "We've always done it that way."
- "If that worked we would be doing it already."
- "We are stretched too thin."

Let's take a quick stroll through these innovation killers. "We tried it and it doesn't work." When I talk about the positive results Philadelphia saw during the Philadelphia Foot Patrol Experiment, I sometimes hear this from officers in cities that tried it. But have they tried to vary the patrols? Change the times? Use different officers? Assign them another way? Your local context may be different, and there are many alternative ways to implement a type of strategy. Avoid this phrase and instead try and think about how the program might be adapted to your area. Then evaluate it.

"We've always done it that way." And frequently, we've always complained about it being done that way. This phrase suggests that nothing has changed in policing since the approach being defended was initiated. It is usually code for a basic unwillingness to take a risk and try something new. Chronic problems will not be solved with traditional tactics.

"If that worked we would be doing it already." Like the previous phrase, this is often code for 'I don't want to do anything new' and masks an assumption that every possible solution has been tried. It also supposes that there are no new problems, yet we know new issues appear with depressing regularity.

"We are stretched too thin." This argument actually has some merit, given the fiscal constraints many police services are under, though it has a logical flaw. If the initiative being suggested is successful, it may reduce calls for service and demand for police services. This will actually free up time and likely save money. This innovation-killing phrase is akin to arguing "We are too busy to do anything to make us less busy."

Develop a good early warning system

Spending time with police leaders has confirmed something Commissioner Charles Ramsey told me years ago: "Police chiefs are used to bad news. They just hate surprises." A regular dose of bad news is almost inevitable in a job such as policing, and command staff (especially in busy urban districts) get used to a certain level of disaster management. It's the unnecessary surprises that tend to get them a little riled up. I'm continually amazed and disappointed in academics who—without warning—release reports that reflect poorly on an agency they work with. When the department castigates them, the academics mistakenly think the police are trying to cover up bad news. All the chief wanted was some advance warning that some negative publicity was imminent.

BOX 11.5 THE IMPORTANCE OF TRACKING WHAT'S GOING ON

"When you scratch beneath the surface, more than anything I have found that what we *say* we do to prevent crime is nothing close to what we *actually* do on the ground. Many of the evidence-based tactics are known widely in policing, such as restorative justice, problem solving and targeting prolific offenders. That's why the importance of tracking what we do is massively underestimated in its value and impact. It's so important to make sure that what is needed is what is actually happening. We have to understand what works and then tirelessly track its implementation and outcome.

Which brings me to the second discovery we have learned from evaluations of police interventions. Quite a lot of what we do backfires, or at best is ineffective. How do we know? Because we use evaluation and track the outcomes. We now know that heavy intrusion on low-risk offenders backfires, as do some mentoring programs, some school interventions, and prosecuting some young low-risk offenders. Everyone is talking about doing more with less but I think this is wrong. Do less with more. Focus on the small amount of things we know work and pursue them ruthlessly with every asset you have."

Alex Murray is currently Assistant Chief Constable (Crime) for West Midlands Police in the U.K. He is Chair of the Society of Evidence-Based Policing.

Many of the partnerships you will need to develop for an effective problem analysis (A in PANDA) will also be useful in identifying emerging issues. Maintain networks that you tap into regularly, even when things are going well. Criminologist Larry Sherman argues that tracking of information and data is essential to evidence-based policing.[11] This point is reinforced by Alex Murray in Box 11.5. It involves an ongoing commitment to monitoring good data on a regular basis, rather than just when a problem emerges. Put systems in place that allow you to circle your area at 'pattern altitude' where you can watch patterns of behavior and information over time. When things change you will be able to assess the change with some context.

It's okay to fail

You probably think this heading is nonsense from an ivory tower academic who doesn't live in the real world. Just about everyone in police management thinks that failure is bad, and in policing failure seems inevitably associated with blame. And blame can damage careers. So we set up organizational and cultural systems to avoid evaluation, promote success (even in the absence of supporting evidence), and vehemently reject criticism.

> Just about everyone in police management thinks that failure is bad, and in policing failure seems inevitably associated with blame.

This culture of blame originates externally (from politicians and the media) but manifests internally. It damages policing, drives risk aversion, and makes everyone defensive, only admitting failure in the relative safety of 'job' pubs and bars. By focusing on blame rather than learning, we train young police commanders to stick rigidly within a narrow range of approved strategies and tactics and disregard more imaginative approaches to the crime problem. They stop using their initiative and common sense.

The rare times when there is an openness to learning from failure, there is a lack of appreciation of how difficult progress really is. Executives (police and otherwise), who should know better, also think that learning from failure is relatively straightforward. Have a quick debrief, promise to do better, and move on. But this hit-and-run approach to learning lessons misses the point. Systems that fail do so because of a long history of tradition, risk aversion, complacency, and conformity. Those systems are harder to change than most folk appreciate. As one superintendent told me "you can fail in policing, as long as you fail conventionally."

Embrace failure as vital to learning what will work in the long term. Think of it this way: We haven't failed, we just haven't succeeded yet. And we usefully learned what doesn't work. Recall the lesson of James Dyson and his prototype vacuums from Chapter 9. Promote a culture that encourages trying new approaches and ways of thinking. You might even choose to reward innovation, even if it isn't eventually successful. Otherwise, we end up with organizations that stagnate. As an inspector in a large police service said to me with a heavy sigh, "We have 180 years of tradition unimpeded by progress."

MANAGING YOURSELF

Resilience

With luck, you will have a long career, so take care of yourself. Command can be rewarding but also stressful. Set reasonable goals for work projects and those around you. This is especially important when working with partner agencies. Because they are not answerable for the level of crime in an area, they can lack the urgency that inhabits policing. That can be stressful, so set realistic expectations for how long they are likely to get their part of any project up and running.

Managing your stress is essential for effective leadership. An established body of research has connected the psychological well-being of staff to job-related outcomes such as individual and organizational productivity. Because crime and other social problems originate outside of policing, this can be tough when we see little improvement in the short term. We should always strive to do as much as we can, but still retain a recognition of the illusion of control (Box 11.6).

> ### BOX 11.6 THE ILLUSION OF CONTROL
>
> The illusion of control is a cognitive bias that fools us into thinking we have complete control as to how a situation will unfold at times when we have no control. Once you have taken all of the available actions that are within your grasp and capacity to control, it is helpful to realize and acknowledge that you have done as much as you can do. Within policing, there are many socio-economic variables that we have no control over, all of which can impact on crime and disorder. Don't use this as an excuse for inaction, but at the same time recognize that finding fault in yourself unnecessarily can lead to frustration and sometimes anger or confusion.[12]

Psychological resilience is "the role of mental processes and behavior in promoting personal assets and protecting an individual from the potential negative effect of stressors."[13] That sounds like something we need more of in policing. There isn't the space in this short book to delve into workplace resilience, but the evidence is increasingly clear that we should all pay attention to our psychological well-being at work.

Keep learning

Policing research and innovation is now happening at a pace never experienced before. For example, the U.K.'s College of Policing has an active research agenda, and the American Society of Criminology has a Division of Policing that has a growing number of scholars and pracademics who are working with police departments on a variety of crime and officer safety projects. We are on the verge of a significant growth in understanding better practices in policing, crime prevention, and officer safety. It's important that you keep yourself (and your colleagues) appraised of the latest developments.

A former boss of mine once neatly summarized the difference between a job and a profession. She said, a profession demands an extra ten hours a week. These aren't necessarily hours at work, but instead time spent reading, thinking, watching work-related videos, undertaking education, attending courses, discussing in online debates, or attending presentations on issues relevant to your profession. If you consider yourself a professional, invest in yourself.

Contribute to the profession

Policing is full of innovation. Regrettably, we learn so little of what good work is taking place. As poet Thomas Gray wrote, "Full many a flower is born to blush unseen, and waste its sweetness on the desert air." We can learn from each other in lots of ways, and it is morale boosting to advertise successes both internally and externally.

It remains the case that most police officers learn from their colleagues and from what neighboring police departments are doing. Try and be less parochial and advertise your successes (and even positive failures that are learning opportunities) not just in department newsletters, but also blogs and social media.

Join a society, like one of the evidence-based policing societies mentioned in the previous chapter. They are full of officers like yourself who are interested in moving policing forward. They have annual meetings where you can learn about innovative approaches to your work. Watching a clip on YouTube is okay, but there is nothing like being in an audience and having the chance to discuss what you learn with neighbors in the meeting with you. And there are usually opportunities to meet with and ask questions of the presenter.

PARTING WORDS

If your role involves taking a new command, you are probably experiencing a range of emotions. Your first days will be a whirlwind of new challenges and it might be easy to forget some of the ideas in this book. Once you settle it, dig it out again and refresh your memory. Like flying an aircraft, policing can be tough to master and sometimes challenging. But it can also afford a view of the world rarely experienced by most people. I hope this book gives you the encouragement to tackle the challenge of reducing crime, improve community safety, and persevere with chronic problems where others have given up. As Inspector Tracey Thompson says at the start of this book: "It's a long journey."

Embrace education, promote evidence-based policing, and keep your institution learning and moving forward. As Thomas Jefferson noted, "Laws and institutions must go hand in hand with the progress of the human mind. As that becomes more developed, more enlightened, as new discoveries are made, new truths disclosed, and manners and opinions change with the change of circumstances, institutions must advance also, and keep pace with the times."[14]

Be safe, and best of luck.

CHAPTER SUMMARY

- There are many leadership styles, including charismatic, situational, appointed, functional, and authentic.
- The functional leader can change approach to meet various demands and needs.
- An authentic leader is someone who exhibits a strong degree of self-awareness and is able to examine their own strengths and weaknesses.
- Adair's action-centered model revolves around the team, the task, and the individual.
- Transactional leadership is suited to day-to-day managers and involves setting goals and using rewards and feedback to drive productivity.
- Transformational leaders think about organizational change, the mission, and are considered more inspirational, exhorting workers to achieve more and seek aspirational goals for the benefits of others.
- Delegation has many benefits for both the leader and the team.
- Strategic and tactical meetings should be part of the Compstat process.
- Keep learning and contribute to the profession.
- If you consider yourself a professional, invest in yourself.

Don't forget that supporting materials are at reducingcrime.com and you can also subscribe to updates on Twitter @_reducingcrime (please note the underscore).

REFERENCES

1 Boon, B., *Blackstone's Leadership for Sergeants and Inspectors*. 2015, Oxford: Oxford University Press.
2 Adair, J., *Action Centred Leadership*. 1973, Maidenhead: McGraw-Hill.
3 Crawford, A. and M. Cunningham, *Working in partnership: The challenges of working across organizational boundaries, cultures, and practices*, in *Police Leadership: Rising to the Top*, J. Fleming, Editor. 2015, Oxford University Press: Oxford. p. 71–94.

4 Davis, C. and D. Bailey, *Police leadership: The challenges for developing contemporary practice*. International Journal of Emergency Services, 2017. **7**(1): p. 13–23.

5 Beech, N., E. Gulledge, and D. Stewart, *Change leadership: The application of alternative models in structural policing changes*, in *Police Leadership: Rising to the Top*, J. FLeming, Editor. 2015, Oxford University Press: Oxford. p. 257–74.

6 Armstrong, M., *Handbook of Human Resource Management Practice (11th edition)*. 2009, London: Kogan Page.

7 Ratcliffe, J.H., *Intelligence-Led Policing (2nd edition)*. 2016, Abingdon, Oxon.: Routledge. **7**(1): p. 13–23.

8 Pease, K. and J. Roach, *How to morph experience into evidence* in *Advances in Evidence-Based Policing*, J. Knutsson and L. Tompson, Editors. 2017, Routledge: New York. p. 84–97.

9 Weisburd, D. and M.K. Majmundar, eds. *Proactive Policing: Effects on Crime and Communities*. 2017, National Academies of Sciences Consensus Study Report: Washington, D.C. p. 2–22.

10 Kunard, L. and C. Moe, *Procedural Justice for Law Enforcement: An Overview*. 2015, Office of Community Oriented Policing Services: Washington, D.C.

11 Sherman, L.W., *Targeting, testing and tracking police services: The rise of evidence-based policing, 1975–2025*, in *Crime and Justice in America, 1975–2025*, M. Tonry, Editor. 2013, University of Chicago Press: Chicago.

12 Langer, E.J., *The illusion of control*. Journal of Personality and Social Psychology, 1975. **32**(2): p. 311–28.

13 Fletcher, D. and M. Sarkar, *Psychological resilience: A review and critique of definitions, concepts, and theory*. European Psychologist, 2013. **18**(1): p. 12–23.

14 Jefferson, T., *Jefferson to H. Tompkinson (AKA Samuel Kercheval)*, in *The Papers of Thomas Jefferson. Retirement series.*, J.J. Looney, Editor. 1816, Princeton University Press: Princeton. p. 226–27.

INDEX

Locators in **bold** refer to tables and those in *italics* to figures.